M000079638

A. J. Liebling A Reporter at Large

DATELINE: PYRAMID LAKE, NEVADA

EDITED, WITH AN UPDATE, BY Elmer R. Rusco

University of Nevada Press / Reno & Las Vegas

University of Nevada Press, Reno, Nevada 89557 USA
Published by arrangement with Russell and Volkening,
agents for the estate of A. J. Liebling.
Originally published in *The New Yorker* (1, 8, 15, 22 January
1955) as "The Lake of the Cui-ui Eaters," copyright © 1955 by
A. J. Liebling, copyright renewed 1983 by Josephine Monsell.
Introduction © copyright 2000 by University of Nevada Press
All rights reserved
Manufactured in the United States of America
Design by Carrie Nelson House

Library of Congress Cataloging-in-Publication Data
Liebling, A. J. (Abbott Joseph), 1904–1964.
   A reporter at large : dateline—Pyramid Lake, Nevada /
A. J. Liebling; edited, with an update, by Elmer R. Rusco.
      p.   cm.
   "Originally published in The New Yorker (1, 8, 15,
22 January 1955) as The lake of the Cui-ui eaters"—
T.p. verso.
   Includes bibliographical references.
   ISBN 0-87417-341-8 (paperback : alk. paper)
      1. Pyramid Lake Indian Reservation (Nev.)—History.
2. Paiute Indians— Government relations.   3. Paiute
Indians—History.   4. Squatters—Nevada—Pyramid
Lake Indian Reservation.   5. Water rights—Nevada—
Pyramid Lake Region.   6. Liebling, A. J. (Abbott
Joseph) (1904–1964)—Journeys—Nevada—Pyramid
Lake Indian Reservation.   I. Rusco, Elmer R.   II. Title.
   E99.P2L53   1999   99-33548
   979.3'55—dc21   CIP
The paper used in this book meets the requirements of
American National Standard for Information Sciences—
Permanence of Paper for Printed Library Materials, ANSI
Z39.48-1984. Binding materials were selected for strength
and durability.

FIRST PRINTING
08 07 06 05 04 03 02 01 00
5 4 3 2 1

Frontispiece: A. J. Liebling and Avery Winnemucca at
the Pyramid Lake Indian Trading Post, 1950s. (Courtesy
of Becky J. Smith)

Contents

Illustrations

Frontispiece: A. J. Liebling and Avery Winnemucca, 1950s

Maps *(in Appendix)*

Introduction

This book brings together for the first time four admirable articles on Pyramid Lake published by noted writer A. J. Liebling in *The New Yorker* in 1955. An introduction and the note on sources at the end of the book have been added to provide more information about Liebling's visits to Nevada—during which he learned about the matters treated in his articles—and to give interested readers a wider and updated context within which his writing can be placed.

Pyramid Lake is located north of Reno in northwestern Nevada. It has long been the ancestral home of what is now the Pyramid Lake Paiute Tribe, aboriginally known to itself and its neighbors as Cui-ui Tucutta, "the Cui-ui Eaters." The cui-ui (pronounced in Northern Paiute something close to coo'ee-oo'ee but by almost all non-Indians and many Indians today as kwee-wee) is a species of fish found uniquely in Pyramid Lake. The annual harvest of the cui-ui, which occurred during the spring spawning run, was for many centuries a major event in tribal life. Cui-ui formerly spawned in very large numbers at the delta of the Truckee River, Pyramid's main source of water.

Former Tribal Chairman Joe Ely has recently described his last participation in this important event, now more than a quarter of a century ago. Tribal members waded into the lake at the delta and harvested large numbers of fish, which could be eaten fresh or dried for use up to two years later.[1]

Today no one—not even Pyramid Lake Paiutes—may fish for cui-ui; it is an endangered species (so declared in 1967), and therefore protected by the federal Endangered Species Act. Only the Tribe's hatchery may remove the cui-ui from the lake, and then only temporarily, as part of the effort to prevent its complete extinction.

Pyramid Lake Paiutes have defined themselves for a long time in terms of the cui-ui; to them, the lake was known as "Cui-ui Pah" or "Cui-ui Water." Joe Ely has written of the "direct relationship between the Cui-ui, the people ('Cui-ui Tucutta'), and the lake ('Cui-ui-Pah' Pyramid Lake). These three creations become the three components that give name and identity to the Pyramid Lake Paiute Tribe. If one component is lost, the identity from creation and an immemorial tradition is completely erased . . . the tribe's past, future and very survival as a people and nation depends on the existence of these three components."

John C. Frémont gave Cui-ui-Pah the name by which it is usually known today, after an impressive, high, tufa-encrusted pyramidal rock rising north of the Truckee River delta along the lake's eastern shore. (Tufa is the name for calcium carbonate deposits formed in the ancient Lake Lahontan—of which Pyramid is a remnant—as the result of chemical reactions initiated by algae. It coats many of the rocks around or in the lake, in various forms and colors.)

Members of Frémont's expedition were probably the first non-Indians to see the lake when they unexpectedly glimpsed it in January 1844. Frémont described his first dramatic encounter with Pyramid Lake: "A sheet of green water . . . broke upon our eyes like the ocean. . . . The waves were curling in the breeze, and their dark-green color showed it to be a body of deep water. For a long time we sat enjoying the view. . . . [Pyramid Lake] was set like a gem in the mountains, which, from our position, seemed to enclose it almost entirely." [2]

The lake's stark beauty has startled and enthralled numerous visitors since the 1840s; to many, it is the most beautiful desert lake in the United States. In 1955 Basil Woon noted what many regular visitors to the lake have experienced when he reported his "customary reverential halt at the top of the hill where the lake first bursts on the eye in all its blinding beauty." [3] More recently, author Mary Webb described one of her many visits to the lake:

> I climb the steep hills; it doesn't take long before a magnificent view of Pyramid Lake blooms between two ridges. I marvel at the perfection in contrasts: burnt umber cliffs, outcroppings of lichen-covered rock, and a broad sweep of valley

that leads to the delft blue of Pyramid Lake. The brilliant water reflects the deep color of the sky, slicing into the beige of the surrounding desert. The lake seems to wear a different shade of blue each time I see it . . . from summer azure to the slate gray and emerald green that often presage a winter storm. In the early light of morning, the lake glitters with excitement, while late afternoon deepens the teal water into a calm expanse. With each season, each hour, Pyramid Lake changes.[4]

To the Pyramid Lake Paiutes, the lake is far more than a beautiful place to experience restorative solitude or marvel at kaleidoscopic displays of color. The waters of the lake sustained aboriginally not only the cui-ui but almost unbelievable quantities of Lahontan cutthroat trout, which could also be taken in the Truckee River all the way to Lake Tahoe. Frémont reported that the flavor of the "salmon trout," which Indians at the delta shared generously with his party, was "superior . . . to that of any fish I have ever known." Basil Woon reported in 1967 that a cui-ui casserole cooked by Joan Drackert for non-Indian guests at the Pyramid Lake Ranch "still waters my palate."[5]

In most years, the spring floods of the Truckee River were sufficient not only to allow spawning of the cui-ui (the trout spawned in streams far above the lake) but also to create wetlands along the shores of Pyramid Lake and in Winnemucca Lake, a shallow basin to the east nearly as extensive in area when full as Pyramid Lake. Cui-ui Pah was an oasis providing the material, as well as spiritual, bases for one of the major Northern Paiute bands, as well as food for surrounding Native American groups.

Most of the land and resources in what became Nevada passed into Anglo-American hands—illegally—at various times from the 1850s to the present. Indeed, this process became complete legally only in 1985, when the United States Supreme Court ruled that the Western Shoshones' belief that most of central Nevada remained under aboriginal ownership could not be litigated. Politically, the Western Shoshones still struggle to assert aboriginal ownership; the Western Shoshone National Council is continuing the effort to have its land claim recognized by Congress, bolstered by the fact that the only court that has ever considered its claim in detail agreed with the Council's contentions.[6]

A few traditionalist Northern Paiutes also believe that their nation still has aboriginal rights to much of its former territory, but there is no concerted effort to assert such rights. Although an appellate judge once agreed that the Paiutes still retain aboriginal ownership, legally it is clear today that the Northern Paiute lands not included in reservations have passed into non-Indian hands, although the Indians were compensated for the loss (at nineteenth-century prices without interest) only recently.[7]

In any case, the Pyramid Lake Tribe has never lost ownership of its lake. In 1859 both Pyramid Lake and Walker Lake (the latter located southeast of Pyramid at the terminus of the Walker River) were created as reservations; presidential executive orders ratifying this action were issued in 1874. The resulting legal status (reservations are held in trust for their Indian owners by the national government) has provided some protection against Anglo-American encroachment, although the Walker River Paiute Tribe lost control of most of its lake as a result of a Congressional statute adopted in 1906.[8]

Some portions of the Pyramid Lake Reservation were occupied by non-Indians at various times; this book recounts some of the controversy resulting from encroachment on the best agricultural lands within the reservation. Nevertheless, the basic integrity of the reservation land base was never lost. The entire lake and most of the land bordering the Truckee River down to the big bend to the west at Wadsworth have never passed out of Indian hands.

More important is the fact that diversion of water from the Truckee River, beginning in a massive way with completion of Derby Dam in 1905, has sharply reduced lake levels. Pyramid Lake dropped eighty-seven feet between 1912 and 1967, and Winnemucca Lake dried up completely (and so far permanently) in 1938. Ironically, the death of Winnemucca Lake came not long after it was declared a national wildlife refuge.[9]

The Lahontan cutthroat trout, once harvested by wagonloads,

became extinct in Pyramid Lake about 1940. The reason in this case was that after Derby Dam was thrown across the river, the trout could no longer reach their upstream spawning grounds. The tribal hatcheries have brought back the trout (because fish of the same species—though not the same variety—still existed in other lakes). The Lahontan cutthroat trout have returned in numbers large enough to sustain a healthy sport fishery, which supplies important income to the Tribe. Nevertheless, natural survival of the trout—without direct human assistance—is still not assured.[10]

The Lahontan cutthroat trout of Pyramid Lake was declared a threatened species in 1975 and has therefore also been brought under federal protection. The cui-ui have been saved from extinction by hatcheries but are still endangered; the chances of their ultimate demise are greater than in the case of the trout. As noted above, no one—not even members of the Tribe—may now procure cui-ui for food.

The Pyramid Lake Paiutes have not been passive observers of these and other assaults on their precious lake. From the Pyramid Lake "War" of 1860 (initially a decisive Indian victory although finally an Indian defeat) to this day, the Pyramid Lake Paiutes have fought back. Today their weapons, in what Liebling calls "the longest-running Indian war in United States history," include legal briefs; testimony by tribal leaders before Congress, legislatures, and administrative agencies; scientific studies to document their lake and seek knowledge of necessary actions; and press releases to make their rights known to the wider community.[11] These recent efforts have been more successful than their earlier violent resistance.

Liebling's important work deals with a portion of this wider conflict—the bitter dispute between the Tribe and non-Indian squatters on the most agriculturally productive lands within the reservation. What makes this story worthy of wide attention is its general significance for understanding Native American/Anglo-American interaction on many levels. It is also important for the light it sheds on the past, present, and future of the state of Nevada.

A. J. Liebling and Nevada

Even if "The Lake of the Cui-ui Eaters" had only literary significance, it would still invite deserved attention; it is stylistically in a class by itself in the literature about Pyramid Lake. A. J. Liebling "may well have been the greatest reporter of his time," as Raymond Sokolov suggested in his biography of this important writer. Liebling's "vigorous, funny, strong" writing, making use of a "flood of irony and metaphor," also dealt in this case with an indisputably serious topic, as did his combat writing during World War II.[12]

Much of Liebling's journalistic output has been collected in books—a total of eighteen before this one. Yet many other pieces, most published in *The New Yorker* after Liebling joined its staff in 1935, remain accessible only in the magazines in which they appeared.

By bringing together Liebling's 1955 articles on Pyramid Lake, the University of Nevada Press has made another part of his wonderful writing available to a wider circle of readers. Since to read Liebling is to laugh and enjoy while learning, this book will surely increase the already large number of his admirers.

A few words are necessary to explain how Liebling came to write on this subject and also to draw attention to other rewarding pieces he wrote about Nevada. In addition, readers will want to know more about some of the individuals he mentions in these articles and about what has happened at Pyramid Lake since he wrote so well about it.

Joe, his name to friends and relatives in spite of the way he signed his work (he did not like Abbott), came to Nevada in 1949 to get a divorce from his first wife, Ann. Although he still loved her, Ann's illness had made their continued marriage impossible, and Joe decided the time had come to end it legally.[13] Facilitating divorce was then a primary means of livelihood for Nevadans, since it brought significant numbers of visitors with enough money to spend six weeks establishing residency in the state.

Joe spent his six weeks at Harry and Joan Drackerts' Pyramid Lake Guest Ranch at Sutcliffe, the second largest community on the reservation, located on the southwestern shore of the lake. He stayed in a house up Hardscrabble Creek above the main complex of cabins at the ranch, because it was a more peaceful place. Liebling's interest in the squatter controversy dates back to this 1949 visit.

Joe's first article about Nevada was published in *The New Yorker* on April 29, 1950, under the title "Slot Machines and Repose." It dealt humorously with several observations Liebling had made about Reno, "that implausible little city (permanent population 21,000)" whose "whole center of town" lay between the railroad tracks and the Truckee River, with the exception of the courthouse, the public library, and the Riverside Hotel, all south of the river. He wrote that "Reno is the only city I am familiar with where you can see fly fishermen in the middle of town, wading in the shallows in pursuit of brook trout, and bait fishermen casting from the bridges for the same delicacy. It is an exhilarating sight." [14]

Joe's reporting from the beginning of his journalistic career highlighted the colorful antics of eccentric characters, particularly those with what he once described as "blarneying capacity." Although "Slot Machines and Repose" does discuss his divorce lawyer, identified only as "the judge," Liebling may have had difficulty finding appropriate Reno characters to describe, because the article begins with an incident that took place in Las Vegas. John F. Cahlan, a regent of the university, had accepted money from gambler Benny Binion to pay the expenses of university athletes, only to have the university's president turn down the offer. Liebling remarked that, although gambling in the state was "as legal . . . as cheesemaking in Wisconsin or being a prophet of God in California," there was "a nuance of respectability between taking money from gamblers and accepting it from them. Reno is alive to nuances." [15]

In spite of the variety of subject matter, his Reno article is vintage Liebling. He commented in his inimitable style about Reno's favorable stance toward the public consumption of alcohol. "Once, walking down Lake Street in Reno at eight o'clock in the morning, I looked in at the door of an old hotel called the Mizpah and saw that the length of the bar, about fifty feet, was packed tightly with battered men and women, elbow to elbow and shoulder to shoulder. . . . I went in, and since I could find no place at the bar, observed them from one end of the room. I ascertained that they had packed themselves together in that fashion in order not to fall down."

While in Reno, Joe was invited to attend the opening of the Desert Inn casino in Las Vegas. His visit to what was then a smaller town than Reno resulted in "Action in the Desert," published in *The New Yorker* on May 13, 1950. This article makes a prescient forecast about the southern Nevada gambling metropolis, noting that "nothing foreseeable can endanger Las Vegas's growth except an acute national depression or the legalization of gambling in California." [16]

Describing Wilbur Clark of the Desert Inn, Liebling wrote that "Clark is especially qualified to be president of the Desert Inn corporation because he has made such an intensive study of goodness. A small man with a pink, young face and gray hair, he has looked into many thousands of other faces in the Far West, always with benevolence. Some faces, he knows, are good for fifty thousand dollars, some are good for only five hundred dollars, and some, even of the fairest, are good for nothing at all."

Liebling's best piece about Las Vegas, however, is "Out Among the Lamisters," published four years later. The point he had made in 1950 about the relationship between the prosperity of Las Vegas and the legal status of gambling in California was put more memorably. He wrote that passage of a bill to legalize gambling in that state "would have cut off Las Vegas's chief source of interstate increment, leaving its businessmen in the plight of landlocked barracuda." [17]

More important, by 1954 Liebling had discovered characters in Las Vegas as fascinating as those New Yorkers he had written about. Sundown Wells, Nick Kelly, and Colonel Jake Friedman are memorable in their own ways, but the star of "Out Among the Lamisters" undoubtedly is Hank Greenspun, editor of the *Las Vegas Sun*. Greenspun had developed the *Sun* from a small sheet begun under labor auspices as part of strike strategy against the *Las*

Vegas Review-Journal into a formidable opponent to the former giant of southern Nevada publishing.

Greenspun had also developed an entirely deserved reputation as a sharp-tongued iconoclast not afraid to take on any foe. He was not even intimidated by the federal government; he was convicted of a federal crime—smuggling arms to the nascent state of Israel—and had been imprisoned for this offense.[18]

By the mid-1950s, Greenspun had realized that Senator Joseph McCarthy was a menace to the Republic. A series of columns attacked McCarthy without quarter. Each was headed with the query: "'Is Senator McCarthy really a secret Communist?'" Liebling remarked: "What makes these pieces exotic blooms in our age is the fine, free-rolling frontier invective that Greenspun, a former lawyer who hails from Brooklyn, drapes over the objects of his scorn. He is an editor-publisher of a type popularly supposed to have gone out with derringer pistols and the Gold Rush."[19]

The feud between Greenspun and McCarthy reached a spectacular peak when the senator visited Las Vegas. During a public address attended by Greenspun, McCarthy accused his foe of being a "confessed Communist." Liebling quotes Greenspun later as saying: "I knew his tongue must have slipped. . . . He runs it too fast anyway. He meant to say 'convict.'"[20]

Greenspun ran to the microphone and challenged McCarthy to stay to debate his allegation. When the senator left the hall without accepting this invitation, Greenspun "launched out on an ad-lib denunciation of lynch law and Fascism. . . . He has been writing rude statements about McCarthy ever since, all libelous per se; if McCarthy sues him, he figures, he can sue McCarthy."

Greenspun did eventually sue Senator Patrick McCarran of Nevada and several Las Vegas casinos, a matter discussed in this book, and eventually won. McCarran was arguably the most powerful Nevada senator at the national level in this century. As chair of the Judiciary Committee and a member of the Appropriations Committee, McCarran could and did coerce numerous federal administrators in pursuit of personal or Nevada interests, as he saw them.[21] One of the senator's victories is noted in this book: he forced the Bureau of Indian Affairs to replace Nevada Indian Superintendent Alida C. Bowler, who had clashed with McCarran on the squatter issue and other questions of Indian rights.

Liebling shrewdly noted in "Out Among the Lamisters" that Senator McCarran's national power rested on maintaining popularity in a rapidly growing Las Vegas, full of newcomers who had not known him since his term on the Nevada Supreme Court or his career as a trial lawyer. Liebling's primary portrait of Senator McCarran is contained in this book and does not need to be discussed further here.

The year before "The Lake of the Cui-ui Eaters," Joe published two articles ("The Mustang Buzzers," in *The New Yorker,* on April 3 and 10, 1954) about hunting wild horses on the Smoke Creek Desert, north of Pyramid Lake. He and his second wife, Lucille, whom he had married in Virginia City after divorcing his first wife, had stayed at the Drackerts' Pyramid Lake Guest Ranch a few months earlier. Ranch records show that Joe arrived on October 20, 1953, and Lucille on November 16. With a few short breaks, they were there until December 10.[22] This nearly two-month stay at Pyramid Lake no doubt was used by Joe to gather most of the materials for what became "The Lake of the Cui-ui Eaters."

"The Mustang Buzzers" moves slowly toward reporting the actual chase and capture of wild horses. Not until the second article does Joe describe how the mustangs were herded by airplane and lured into corrals by domesticated horses. This second article ends with a dramatic description of the capture of a wild stallion who nearly escapes and Lucille's unsuccessful plea that his life be saved. Liebling is ambivalent about the fate of the stallion. After saying that the animal had a "wild and noble" head, he remarked: "I felt a bit blue myself, but I can't explain why. There was nothing friendly about the old stud." When invited to come back for more mustang hunting the next day, however, Joe declined with the comment: "I thought I had the general idea."[23] Since then, the hunting of wild mustangs to feed dogs has come to an end: Lucille's viewpoint has become national policy.

My wife, Mary, and I met Lucille Liebling in the fall of 1963, while she was living in Wadsworth. She had divorced Joe in 1955 (staying at the Pyramid Lake Guest Ranch with her daughter, Susan Spectorsky, from August 2, 1955, to September 8).[24] Lucille was deeply interested in Indians; Mary met her while both were attending a class on Great Basin Indians at the University of Nevada. We visited her in Wadsworth and went with her once to observe wild flowers in Olinghouse Canyon with a Pyramid Lake Paiute Indian woman. Lucille told us that Arthur Miller's screenplay for the film *The Misfits* was "my story."

The movie also reports the dramatic capture of a wild stallion and concludes with the successful effort of the heroine (played by Marilyn Monroe) to save him and the other captured mustangs. Arthur Miller, in describing the origin of his screenplay, says nothing about Liebling's article. Instead, he reports learning about mustanging from two unnamed practitioners of that trade whom he met at the Stix Ranch, south of Pyramid Lake. It is highly likely that these were Hugh Marchbank and Bill Garaventa, the chief protagonists of Liebling's mustang articles, because Miller visited Pyramid Lake about a year after Joe and Lucille's long sojourn.[25] Presumably the two mustangers told Miller about the incident concluding Liebling's articles.

The Lake of the Cui-ui Eaters: The Cast of Characters

"The Mustang Buzzers" also introduces Harry and Joan Drackert, proprietors of the Pyramid Lake Guest Ranch at the time of Joe's visits. Harry, originally a Montana cowboy, traveled the rodeo circuit for nearly a decade and earned the title of "Cowboy of America" at Madison Square Garden. In 1931 he moved to Reno; after defecting to the San Francisco Bay Area during World War II, he returned to Reno and managed the Mount Rose Guest Ranch before moving on to Pyramid Lake. From 1947 to 1956, he was the proprietor of the Pyramid Lake Guest Ranch.[26]

Harry was evidently more interested in breeding racehorses and hunting than in operating a ranch whose principal customers were eastern divorcees. The first "Mustang Buzzers" article describes a Canada geese hunt that took place partly at Fish Springs Ranch, which was in the news in Reno during 1993–1994, when its owner at that time wished to export water from the ranch to the Truckee Meadows, for a tidy profit.

Joan Drackert was ten years younger than Harry. She is described accurately by Joe as "a blonde with a good figure and an inquiring mind, and her wide gray eyes were slightly keener than a chicken hawk's." [27] Her sharp eyesight no doubt aided her in her hobby of trapshooting; she eventually won three state championships in that sport.

Joan wrote in a brief autobiographical statement, probably composed in 1989, that as a teenager she had spent summers in Evergreen, Colorado, where she "learned to ride—fell in love with Floyd, the wrangler—a Colorado Aggie's student—& the West, forever!" Unlike her love for the West, her attachment to Floyd must have been transient. She came to Reno in 1946 to divorce her first husband, a Major Deeley, and became a hostess at a guest ranch. When Harry moved to Pyramid Lake, Joan went along as the ranch hostess, and they married in 1950. She efficiently managed the business side of the ranch and three subsequent guest ranches in the Truckee Meadows, which the Drackerts operated after they left Pyramid Lake.[28]

The Pyramid Lake Guest Ranch had a trading post selling Pyramid Lake Paiute arts and crafts, among other things. An undated price list for the trading post lists buckskin jackets ($70–$90), completely beaded buckskin moccasins ($2–$30), buckskin gloves ($5–$35), plus beaded coin purses, bags, cigarette cases, belts, necklaces, wrist bands, and buttons (for prices ranging from $2 to $25). All of these were probably of local origin, although the store also sold Navajo rugs and southwestern pottery. The same price list includes "Antique Paiute Baskets" for $4 to $20 apiece. Liebling describes in these articles seeing Joan Drackert wearing a dress, trimmed with beads, which was made by Nellie Calico, a member of the Pyramid Lake Paiute Tribe.

After the Drackerts' move to Reno, Joan managed not only guest ranches but Indian Territory, a shop in downtown Reno (next to the First National Bank Building at First and Virginia) from 1971 to 1986. This excellent store sold numerous items made by Nevada Indians, especially members of the Pyramid Lake Paiute Tribe.

In "The Lake of the Cui-ui Eaters," Joe says that he acquired significant information about the squatter controversy from a 1944 publication of the Bureau of Indian Affairs. After first hearing about the issue from Pyramid Lake Indians whom he met in Sutcliffe, he searched the library at the guest ranch for further information and found this document.

Joe met several tribal members at the Drackerts' bar, which Harry often pointed out had "the only obtainable liquor license on the entire lake." (Indeed, it was the only bar between Reno and Gerlach, a distance of 120 miles.) In "The Mustang Buzzers," Liebling tells his readers about "Paiute Poker," "a three-card game in which you play for the ante, but as it warms, players challenge each other with side bets, until you find yourself with stakes on high card, high spade, low spade, high heart, low club, and anything else that occurs to anybody." [29]

Joe also describes meeting several Pyramid Lake Paiutes. The first real Indian he met was Martin Greene (not Green, as Liebling reports it), a tribal policeman on the reservation. In "The Mustang Buzzers," he mentions that Bill Garaventa, the pilot of the mustanging plane, had once seen Greene wearing a fur coat while chasing a camel on the reservation. Garaventa learned later that Greene had been portraying "a fierce Mongol horseman" for a film about the Gobi Desert which was being filmed at the lake. [30]

Martin was the son of Joe and Bessie Winnemucca Greene. Anthropologist Omer Stewart once published an article describing Joe Greene's prominence as an Episcopal lay reader (there has long been an Episcopal mission at Nixon). But Stewart noted that Greene was also a Northern Paiute shaman and a road chief for the Native American (or peyote) church. [31]

Martin was born in 1913, graduated from Carson Indian School, and was a policeman for the school from 1941 to 1943. During World War II he served twenty-seven months as a military policeman, dealing mostly with German prisoners of war. In 1945 Martin Greene returned to the Pyramid Lake Reservation as the tribal police officer. He died in 1955.[32]

Other Pyramid Lake Indians mentioned by Joe include Levi Frazier and his wife, Grace, Avery Winnemucca, Harry Winnemucca, Warren Tobey, Abe and Sue Abraham, Ted James, and Albert Aleck. Levi Frazier Sr. is described by Liebling as "the best roper on the Pyramid Lake Reservation." Frazier was well known as a horse trainer; animals he had trained won many races at Bay Meadows and other California tracks. He was the first full-blooded Indian to be awarded a gold card by the Rodeo Cowboy Association. Levi's widow, Grace, still lived at Pyramid Lake at the end of 1998.[33]

Avery and Harry Winnemucca were descendants of nineteenth-century Northern Paiute leader Chief Winnemucca (after whom the Nevada city of Winnemucca is named). Avery, a long-time tribal leader, is described by Joe as the Tribe's "most oratorical spokesman." He was chairman of the Tribal Council in the early 1950s, when the squatter controversy was at its height. The struggle at this point had become complicated by the successful move of the Bureau of Indian Affairs to cancel the Tribe's contract with its attorney, James Curry. Avery Winnemucca led a delegation to Washington, D.C., in the fall of 1951 to defend tribal interests on both of these matters.[34]

Warren Tobey, another tribal leader, played an important role in restoring the Lahontan cutthroat trout fishery and saving the cui-ui from extinction. He was also a member of the Tribal Council in the 1950s. Abe and Sue Abraham (originally Mauwee) were the proprietors of the first Indian-owned store at Nixon. For about fifteen years (from 1946 to 1970), Abe and Sue sold groceries, ranch supplies, and hardware and became well known in northwestern Nevada. Sue continued to live in Sutcliffe after Abe's death, until she died in the 1990s.[35]

Ted James, a rancher, played a prominent role in establishing the first contemporary tribal council based on a written constitution; from 1934 to 1936 he was the secretary of this council. He was the father of Alvin James, who in 1993 was elected chairman of the

Pyramid Lake Paiute Tribe, and of Robert James, who was also a member of the Tribal Council in 1993. Albert Aleck was the father of Alan Aleck, in 1993 a member of the Tribal Council. In 1950 Albert Aleck was chairman of the Pyramid Lake Paiute Tribal Council.[36]

Liebling was noted for his fabulous memory and consequently accurate reporting, despite his marvelously humorous flights of fancy. Only three factual corrections need to be made today. Not one of these is consequential; in one case, Joe did not have available to him current knowledge about the question. The correct spelling of the Greene family name has been noted above. Liebling also says that there is an "underground" entrance to Winnemucca Lake from Pyramid Lake. The above-ground Winnemucca Slough ran between Marble Bluff and a ridge to the north; the highway to Gerlach now cuts across and dams it.[37]

Finally, Liebling wrote that the Pyramid Lake Paiutes had lived at the lake for 3,500 years. The present state of knowledge in this area is that Native Americans have lived around Pyramid Lake for 11,000–12,000 years. One theory, however, is that they did not arrive until around 800–1,000 years ago, as part of a general expansion of Numic-speaking people into the Great Basin. This hypothesis is largely based on linguistic analysis, and there is today no consensus on its validity.[38]

In any case, the inhabitants of Pyramid Lake when Frémont became the first Anglo-American to see it were the descendants of people who had lived there for a very long time in relation to the century and a half after Frémont, during which other Americans have lived in what became Nevada.

Pyramid Lake Today

How much Liebling knew about the legal status of the Pyramid Lake Paiute Tribe is not clear. Although he does not mention attending Tribal Council meetings, many of the Indians he identifies by name were elected tribal leaders. It is important in understanding the articles he wrote and what has happened since to know that the Tribe shares a unique legal standing with other recognized Native American societies. Although this status has been eroded in recent decades, in U.S. law the governments of these societies are inheritors of the sovereignty that their ancestral nations possessed before European entry. In the most important Supreme Court decision defining the status of these societies—with which the United States government made treaties until 1871—Chief Justice John Marshall wrote that

> the Indian nations had always been considered as distinct, independent, political communities. . . . The constitution, by declaring treaties already made, as well as those to be made, to be the supreme law of the land, . . . admits their rank among those powers who are capable of making treaties. The words "treaty" and "nation," are words of our own language. . . . We have applied them to Indians, as we have applied them to the other nations of the earth; they are applied to all in the same sense.[39]

Marshall also said that European nations, and later the United States, had acquired the authority to regulate the dealings of Native Americans with other nations and also the right to extinguish aboriginal property rights (though not arbitrarily). Later, the Supreme Court held that Congress has plenary—or full—power to abrogate the sovereign status of Indian nations. Yet Congress has never done this in any sweeping fashion, although it did "terminate" a few societies during a short period after World War II. Several of these societies have since regained their prior legal status.[40]

One aspect of this unique legal status is that states have only the authority over tribes that is given to them by the U.S. government. Since the national Constitution and the laws and treaties promulgated under its authority are "the supreme law of the land," the national government has almost exclusive authority in Indian affairs. Most decisions affecting Indian societies, down to the present, are made by Indian governments or the national government.

The Pyramid Lake Paiute Tribe, as noted above, has vigorously defended its interests and the preservation of Pyramid Lake for many decades. These efforts, particularly the Tribe's persistent and skillful use of the federal courts (thanks in substantial measure to longtime tribal attorney Robert S. Pelcyger), have been increasingly successful. Two legal victories have been of crucial importance in protecting the lake.

First, the Tribe has won several rulings that have reduced substantially the diversions of water at Derby Dam to the Lahontan Valley—the site of the federal reclamation project whose opening led to greatly reduced flows to Pyramid Lake. Second, in 1982 it won federal court decisions holding that Stampede Reservoir (located on a tributary of the Truckee River in the Sierra Nevada) must be operated solely to protect the endangered cui-ui and the threatened Lahontan cutthroat trout.[41]

In 1990 Congress passed a comprehensive statute, the Truckee–Carson–Pyramid Lake Water Rights Settlement Act, which if implemented will ensure enough water for the survival of Pyramid Lake, although not at the levels often reached before Euro-American settlement of Nevada. This complex statute has many elements, including restoration of the wetlands of the Lahontan Valley (where the white pelicans who live on Anaho Island in Pyramid Lake often feed).[42]

Several features of the law provide benefits to Pyramid Lake. For one, the Secretary of the Interior is mandated to restore the fisheries for both species of fish protected by the Endangered Species Act. This will require the acquisition of additional water rights for this purpose, beyond those already won by the Tribe. In addition, the Tribe must win from the state of Nevada a legal right acceptable to its government to the remaining unappropriated waters of the Truckee River—essentially the waters now flowing to Pyramid Lake in very wet years because there is insufficient storage capacity to hold them back.[43] Beyond this, the federal government is authorized to purchase water rights needed for restoration of the fisheries. Finally, purchases of lands and water rights within the reservation are authorized.

As of the beginning of 1999, it was not absolutely certain, but extremely likely, that the Negotiated Settlement, as it is called, would go into effect. The State Engineer of Nevada has issued two rulings on the unappropriated Truckee waters, assigning these to the Tribe and denying other applications. However, the latest ruling placed a ceiling on the annual amount of the flood-water right and left pending two potentially competing applications. Various agencies of the national and Nevada governments as well as private groups—including the Nature Conservancy and the American Land Conservancy—are working with the Tribe to carry out the intent of the settlement.

Most elements of the settlement are already in place, although approved plans for the recovery of both species of fish and new operating rules for the Truckee River had yet to be completed by the end of February 1999. On May 2, 1993, the Pyramid Lake Paiute Tribe celebrated the first spawning run of the cui-ui in six years. In October 1995, in a cooperative program between national and state wildlife agencies and the Pyramid Lake Paiute Tribe, 30,000 Lahontan cutthroat trout fingerlings were released into the Truckee River, from which they had been absent for more than forty years.[44] There has also been substantial progress toward purchase of water rights for restoration of the wetlands in Lahontan Valley.[45]

The struggle to save Pyramid Lake will not be over until the lake level is stabilized and the cui-ui and Lahontan cutthroat trout are restored to population levels not requiring hatcheries to sustain them. When and if this happens, the third element of the factors involved in the long-term identity of the Pyramid Lake Paiutes will have been restored.

The Friends of Pyramid Lake have assisted in the publication of this book, featuring the articles by A. J. Liebling that first appeared in *The New Yorker* in 1955. Help in preparing this introduction and the note on sources was provided by Day Williams, Leslie Gray, Joy Leland, Jo Anne Peden, Robert S. Pelcyger, Marjorie Sill, William Isaeff, and the staffs of the Special Collections Department at the University of Nevada, Reno, Library and the Nevada State Historical Society. Peden's help was especially important, because she alerted us to photographs displayed in the tribal museum at Sutcliffe, which appear in this book. Readers will note that chapters two through four begin with summaries of the previous essay, because they were not published all at once. But this in no way detracts from the literary or historical value of these fine articles.

Notes

1. Joe Ely, "More Than Romance," in Peter Goin, Robert Dawson, and Jill Winter (eds.), *Dividing Desert Waters, Nevada Public Affairs Review* 1 (1992): 60–63. The quotation just below is on p. 62.

2. John Charles Frémont, *Report of the Exploring Expedition to the Rocky Mountains* (Ann Arbor: University Microfilms, 1966), 216.

3. Basil Woon, *Nevada State Journal*, 6 March 1955, 8.

4. Mary Webb, "Pyramid Lake: The Tonic of Wilderness," in *Dividing Desert Waters*, 52.

5. See John M. Townley, *The Truckee Basin Fishery, 1844–1944* (Reno: Desert Research Institute, Water Resources Center, Publication No. 43008), for a history of this fishery. Frémont, *Report of the Exploring Expedition*, 174; Basil Woon, *None of the Comforts of Home: The Saga of the Nevada Dude Ranches* (Reno: Federated Features, 1967), 24.

6. See Elmer R. Rusco, "Historic Change in Western Shoshone Country: The Establishment of the Western Shoshone National Council," *American Indian Quarterly* 16, no. 3 (summer 1992): 337–60.

7. Opinion by Judge Nichols of U.S. Court of Claims, in *U.S. vs. Northern Paiute Nation*, 183 Ct. Cl. 321, 353, 358 (1968).

8. Edward C. Johnson, *Walker River Paiutes: A Tribal History* (Salt Lake City: University of Utah Printing Service, 1975).

9. Gary P. Horton, *Truckee River Chronology* (Carson City: Division of Water Planning, 1995), 3:15, 10.

10. Because the Nevada Wildlife Division had transplanted Lahontan cutthroat trout from Pyramid Lake before their extinction there, at least one remnant of the population that used to inhabit Pyramid Lake may be still in existence. The Lahontan National Fish Hatchery in Gardnerville, Nevada, has been raising fish from this population for several years. Patrick C. Trotter, *Cutthroat: Native Trout of the West* (Boulder, Col.: Colorado Associated University Press, 1987), 118–22; personal communications to the author from Nancy Vucinich, 16 August 1998, and Larry Marchant, 28 August 1998, 2 September 1998.

11. See William C. Miller, "The Pyramid Lake Indian War of 1860,"

Nevada Historical Society Quarterly 1, no. 1 (1957): 37–53, and 1, no. 2 (1957): 98–113; Ferol Egan, *Sand in a Whirlwind: The Paiute Indian War of 1860* (Garden City, N.Y.: Doubleday, 1972).

12. Raymond Sokolov, *Wayward Reporter: The Life of A. J. Liebling* (New York: Harper and Row, 1980), ix, 13.

13. Ibid., 95, 124–26.

14. A. J. Liebling, "Slot Machines and Repose," *The New Yorker*, 29 April 1950, p. 86 for both quotations.

15. Sokolov, *Wayward Reporter*, 146; Liebling, "Slot Machines and Repose," 86, 92. The following quotation is on p. 86.

16. A. J. Liebling, "Action in the Desert," *The New Yorker*, 13 May 1950, 106. The following quotation is on p. 111.

17. A. J. Liebling, "Out Among the Lamisters," *The New Yorker*, 27 March 1954, 74.

18. See Hank Greenspun (with Alex Pelle), *Where I Stand* (New York: David McKay Co., 1966); and Jake Highton, *Nevada Newspaper Days: A History of Journalism in the Silver State* (Stockton, Calif.: Heritage West Books, 1990), 233–52.

19. Liebling, "Out Among the Lamisters," 74.

20. Ibid., 78.

21. The fullest account of this episode is in Michael S. Green, "The Las Vegas Newspaper War of the 1950s," *Nevada Historical Society Quarterly* 31, no. 3 (fall 1988): 155–82. See also Greenspun, *Where I Stand*; Highton, *Nevada Newspaper Days*, 236–37. Jerome E. Edwards, *Pat McCarran: Political Boss of Nevada* (Reno: University of Nevada Press, 1982) discusses McCarran's career, with emphasis on his impact on Nevada. A full-length study of the senator's national role is needed.

22. The first article has been reprinted in James Barber and Fred Warner (eds.), *Liebling at the New Yorker* (Albuquerque: University of New Mexico Press, 1994), 132–47, and the second in William Cole (ed.), *The Most of A. J. Liebling* (New York: Simon and Schuster, 1963), 293–303. Harry and Joan Drackert deposited their joint papers in the Special Collections Department, Getchell Library, University of Nevada, Reno. Series 1, Box 1 of this collection contains "Pyramid Lake Guest Ranch, Financial Ledger, 1950–1955," which has detailed information on dates of residence of guests during this period.

23. Liebling, "The Mustang Buzzers," *The New Yorker*, 3 and 10 April 1954, I: 85.

24. Drackert Papers, Financial Ledger.

25. See James Goode, *The Story of "The Misfits"* (New York: Bobbs-Merrill Co., 1963). Basil Woon says that Marchbank had changed his name from Marjoribanks, "a family prominent in England these many centuries" (Woon, *None of the Comforts of Home*, 30).

26. Drackert Papers, Financial Ledger. Additional information about the Drackerts can be found in Woon, *None of the Comforts of Home,* and *Reno Evening Gazette,* 7 Oct. 1984, F1. Information about the predecessors of the resort can be found in the papers of Mary Bean, in Special Collections, Getchell Library, University of Nevada, Reno.

27. Liebling, "The Mustang Buzzers," I: 35.

28. Data on the Drackerts are from the Drackert Papers, especially Susan Searcy, "A Guide to the Papers of Harry and Joan Drackert" (1991), and the sources cited above.

29. Liebling, "The Mustang Buzzers," I: 38, 35.

30. Ibid., II: 70, 72.

31. Omer C. Stewart, "Three Gods for Joe," *Tomorrow* 4, no. 3 (1956): 71–76.

32. Flora Greene (sister of Martin Greene), interviews by Elmer R. Rusco, 20 July 1993, 10 August 1993.

33. *Nevada State Journal,* 18? November? 1973, in Joy Leland Papers, Special Collections, Getchell Library, University of Nevada, Reno; Grace Frazier (widow of Levi Frazier Sr.), interviews by Elmer R. Rusco, 20 July 1993, 10 August 1993.

34. For studies of the attorney controversy, see Stanley J. Underdal, "On the Road to Termination: The Pyramid Lake Paiutes and the Indian Attorney Controversy of the 1950s" (Ph.D. diss., Columbia University, 1977); and Richard Drinnon, *Keeper of Concentration Camps: Dillon S. Myer and American Racism* (Berkeley: University of California Press, 1987), 175–213.

35. Drinnon, *Keeper of Concentration Camps,* 186, 264; *Federal Protection of Indian Resources: Hearings,* Part 6, Subcommittee on Administrative Practice and Procedure, U.S. Senate Judiciary Committee, 92d Cong., 1st Session (Washington, D.C., 1972); Warren Tobey, interview by Elmer R. Rusco, 28 July 1988; Sue Abraham, interview by Elmer R. Rusco, 5 January 1993.

36. Elmer R. Rusco, "Formation of the Pyramid Lake Paiute Tribal Council, 1934–1936," *Journal of California and Great Basin Anthropology* 10, no. 22 (1988): 187–208; Althea Blossom (daughter of Ted James), interview by Elmer R. Rusco, 10 August 1993; Martha C. Knack and Omer C. Stewart, *As Long as the River Shall Run: An Ethnohistory of the Pyramid Lake Indian Reservation* (Berkeley: University of California Press, 1984), 261.

37. George Hardman and Cruz Venstrom, "A 100-Year Record of Truckee River Runoff Estimated from Changes in Levels and Volumes of Pyramid and Winnemucca Lakes," *Transactions* of the American Geophysical Union (1941): 73, 77.

38. See David B. Madsen and David Rhode (eds.), *Across the West:*

Human Population Movement and the Expansion of the Numa (Salt Lake City: University of Utah Press, 1994).

39. *Worcester v. Georgia*, 31 U.S. 515 (1832): 559.

40. See Felix S. Cohen, *Handbook of Federal Indian Law* (Charlottesville, Va.: Michie Bobbs-Merrill, 1982).

41. *Carson-Truckee Water Conservancy District et al. v. James G. Watt*, 537 Fed. Supp. 106, and District Court Judgment in this case dated 22 October 1982, in which the Secretary of the Interior was ordered to "utilize the waters stored in Stampede Reservoir for the benefit of the Pyramid Lake Fishery until such time as the cui-ui and Lahontan cutthroat trout are no longer classified as endangered or threatened species or until sufficient water becomes available from other sources to conserve the cui-ui and Lahontan cutthroat trout."

42. See Elmer R. Rusco, "The Truckee–Carson–Pyramid Lake Water Rights Settlement Act and Pyramid Lake," *Dividing Desert Waters*, 9–15.

43. In August 1998 the Nevada State Engineer denied the 1930 application of the Truckee-Carson Irrigation District for a right to the flood waters of the Truckee. TCID was then the primary applicant for this right other than the Pyramid Lake Paiute Tribe. See "In the Matter of Application 9330 . . . ," Ruling 4659, Office of the State Engineer of the State of Nevada, 14 August 1998. In November 1998 the State Engineer ruled that the Pyramid Lake Paiute Tribe had the right to unappropriated waters of the Truckee River, but limited this right to 477,851 acre feet annually. "In the Matter of Applications . . . Filed to Appropriate the Waters of the Truckee River and its Tributaries . . . ," Ruling 4683, Office of the State Engineer of the State of Nevada, 24 November 1998. The Cities of Reno and Sparks plus Washoe County and the Sierra Pacific Power Company decided in December 1998 not to appeal this decision. Katy Simon et al., to Chairman Mervin Wright and Tribal Council, 24 December 1998; William Isaeff, interview by Elmer R. Rusco, 19 February 1999.

44. *Reno Gazette-Journal*, 18 Oct. 1995, D1.

45. Jo Anne Peden, interview by Elmer R. Rusco, 20 November 1995; tribal official Sharon Keever, interview by Elmer R. Rusco, 20 November 1995; tribal official Randy Tobey, interview by Elmer R. Rusco, 6 December 1995; *Newsletter of American Land Conservancy* (winter/spring 1995): 4; John Jackson, Director of Water Resources of the Pyramid Lake Paiute Tribe, interview by Elmer R. Rusco, 22 February 1999; Alvin James, interview by Elmer R. Rusco, 22 February 1999. Mr. Jackson supplied the map of agricultural lands on the Pyramid Lake Reservation today.

The Lake of the Cui-ui Eaters

1

When I first set eyes on Pyramid Lake, in Nevada, in July, 1949, I knew as little about it as Captain John C. Frémont, its official discoverer, did when he first spied it, in January, 1844. He had been informed of the lake's imminent apparition by his guides, a couple of Bannock Indians, and I by my guide, a fellow named Wallie Warren, who ordinarily directed the public relations of a gambling house in Reno. Even though forewarned, Frémont must have been astonished by his first view of a hundred and twenty thousand acres of changeable blue water in the middle of a ring of desert mountains. I know I was. The lake is shaped like a harp, thirty-one miles on its longest axis, with the narrow end south. It is ten or eleven miles across the wide end, and its water, when you swim in it, has the soothing quality of a cool solution of boric acid, while in the mouth it tastes like Alka-Seltzer gone flat. It thus affords the greatest double-action hangover cure known to man, and were it possible to transport sufferers from their beds of pain to the lakeside before their affliction subsided, Pyramid might become one of the great spas of the world. The water, approximating, I should judge, the specific gravity of the Baltic Sea, is more buoyant than the strictly fresh kind, less so than the oceanic variety. Like many solitary lakes, it is reputed to have a bottomless spot and a species of fish found nowhere else. Nobody has yet come upon the first, although I was told that Navy hydrographers have sounded to twelve hundred feet at one place. The lake does, however, hold a species of fish—*Chasmistes cujus*—that isn't found anywhere else but has relatives in certain lakes of India, Utah, and eastern Oregon. The flesh, when smoked, tastes like a mediocre grade of sturgeon, and Chasmistes possesses a share of the sturgeon's anachronistic ugliness. By circumstantial evidence that satisfies some geologists, the lake is only about thirty-two hundred years old—a calculation based in part on the amount of salts in the water of the Truckee River, its only feeder. Water evaporates, but the salts just accumulate, and a gallon of Pyramid Lake water compared with a gallon of Truckee River water produces this answer. In spite of the lake's callow youth, however, the depression it occupies has yielded remains of prehistoric animals of species that were considered much less recent until these bones were discovered, and it may be that the Paiute Indians once had to contend with the American mastodon. A workout with a mastodon would have been a useful form of training for the struggle I found them engaged in with the late United States Senator Patrick A. McCarran, a neighbor of theirs, as Nevada distances go. The struggle was—and is, for the issues behind it are still operative, despite the demise of one party to the dispute—the contemporary phase of the longest continuous Indian war in the history of the United States, beginning with open hostilities in 1860, continuing through the administrations of twenty-seven Indian commissioners, and requiring the attention of the United States District Court and the United States Circuit Court of Appeals.

In citing the following details, I outrun my narrative, but I wish to establish the lake in the reader's mind as a body of water of magnitude and originality. In it are a number of curiously shaped islets of tufa, a chalky sediment precipitated from the water by an alga, which thus raises an impressive memorial to itself. The alga operates in a way that is not precisely like that of the coral animal, but the effect is rather similar. A group of these tufa domes near the northwest corner of the lake resembles a reëmergent town, its population drowned and its architectural detail erased. Frémont, coming upon the lake from the mountains above its southeastern extremity, was struck by the appearance of a less remarkable tufa islet, just off that shore, which, he wrote in his journal, "from the point we viewed it, presented a pretty exact outline of the great pyramid of Cheops." He accordingly named the whole hundred-and-twenty-thousand-acre expanse of water Pyramid Lake. The Paiutes had called it the Lake of the Cui-Ui, which was Chasmistes' name before the taxonomists got to work, and, indeed, the Paiutes who lived near the lake were known to their fellow-tribesmen elsewhere as "the cui-ui eaters," although, as Frémont soon learned, they also had better fish to fry. When he arrived at the lake, after a march across frightening desert country, he met up with a band of Paiutes, who presented him and his men with a number of what he termed salmon trout, and they proved to be a delicious change from jerky and biscuit. They were, in fact, cutthroat trout, a species named for the red gill slashes just behind their heads. "They were of extraordinary size —about as large as the Columbia River salmon—generally from two to four feet in length," Frémont wrote. Of his benefactors, he reported, "These Indians were very fat, and appeared to live an easy and happy life." To spawn, the trout swam up a little river that flowed into the southern end of the lake, and Frémont named this the Salmon-Trout River. Unlike Pyramid Lake, the designation failed to catch the mapmakers' fancy. The same year, another party of whites called it Truckee River, for a Paiute chief, and the name has endured.

Between Frémont's arrival and mine, a number of changes had occurred in and around Pyramid Lake, none of them discernible to a newcomer. The surface of the lake had dropped about fifty feet, leaving beaches in places. The great cutthroat trout had disappeared, because they could no longer get across the shallows at the river's mouth to spawn. The Indians were therefore less fat. But in general the lake looked now as it must have then—alone among the hills and without a boat on it. The hills themselves are black, beige, tawny, pink, or purple, according to the light on them. The only color they never are is green, because they are naked. The lake runs through all the tones of turquoise, with the blues at one end of the gamut and the greens at the other, but it never appears unfrightening. My friend Martin Green, a Paiute who crossed the Atlantic many times during the war as a military policeman guarding prisoners, says he liked to lie on the deck of the Queen Elizabeth and look down at the water, because it reminded him of the lake. He also says that when you dive deep in the middle of the lake, you feel something trying to keep you down, and you have to kick hard to break its grip.

My own approach to Pyramid Lake was from the south —the direction of Reno. I was bound for the lake because I had found it necessary to become a resident of Nevada for at least six weeks, and two nights in the Biggest Little City in the World had indicated to me that if I stayed there I might not last the distance. I had counted on doing a bit of writing while in limbo, and so far it had all been on American Express checks. Also, I am a zero player; there were zeros on the Reno roulette wheels, but they never turned up. I explained my apprehensions to my Nevada attorney, and he, grasping the fact that his fee might depend on my leaving Reno quickly, advised "a ranch." My attorney was addressed as Judge, as are half the members of the Nevada bar. This is because Nevada is a state of small population but numerous courts. There are seventeen counties, several with a population of fewer than a thousand, and the demand for both judges and district attorneys is steady. Distances preclude the amalgamation of jurisdictions; the state is bigger than New York and North Carolina put together. Young lawyers often begin their legal careers as judges and then move to Reno or Las Vegas, where they can earn a living as lawyers. My man had been district attorney and then judge in White Pine County, on the eastern border of the state, which is three hundred and fifty miles in a beeline from Reno. I used to call my judge the White Pine Blackstone. In Ely, the county seat of White Pine, he had perforce specialized in homicide cases, which were the only ones permitted to reach trial, because of an overcrowded calendar. He had prospered in Reno, but he sometimes spoke nostalgically of this more decisive early practice. White Pine is a mining county with severe winters, and during the cold weather the miners used to get on one another's nerves, and also on their wives', if they happened to have any. Those who got on their wives' nerves made a big mistake, the Judge said, because there were many more men than women around, and an abused wife had a pretty good chance of improving her situation if widowed. "A husband should never become presumptuous under such circumstances," he told me. The Judge was a square-shouldered gentleman with white hair and a genial manner that made his occasional didactic tendencies tolerable. "I remember one cold, clear night when I was district attorney," he said. "I was walking home about twelve o'clock." I did not

4

ask him where he had been. "There was a light in the house of a couple I shall call Simpson, and presently I heard a shot. The lack of counterfire indicated that it had been fatal, so I said to myself, 'Never put off until tomorrow what you can do today.' I knocked and walked in. Doors were never locked in White Pine then, for we were honest people. Sitting on the edge of the double bed in her nightgown was Mrs. Simpson, whom I knew well. By her was a revolver, which I assumed she had just discarded. 'Hello, Bill,' she said. 'What brings you around here?' 'I must apologize for the hour, Emily,' I said, 'but I just happened to be passing. Tell me what occurred.' 'Oh,' she said, 'we were arguing, as usual, before turning out the lamp, and he reached over by his side of the bed and brought up a gun and pointed it at me. I grabbed it, and somehow it went off and killed him.' 'Emily,' I said, 'that won't do. Look at the side of the bed he is on, and we both know he wasn't left-handed. You better get some clothes on and come along with me down to the jail. I'll send out for the matron.' We were strong on propriety. 'But if you'd just killed him last week, when he beat the hell out of you,' I said, 'you could have pleaded self-defense and I wouldn't even have had to hold you on bail.'"

The judge and I were talking in the apple-green corner bar of the Riverside Hotel, where he often held consultations, and when he had finished telling me about Mrs. Simpson, he introduced me to a fellow named Harry Drackert, who, he said, had been the national bronc-riding champion back in the twenties—both Harry's and the century's. Mr. Drackert, it developed, conducted a guest ranch on the western side of Pyramid Lake, about thirty miles from town, and it was from his lips that I had my first inkling of the lake's scenic glories. All the guests at the ranch were people who, like me, had decided to become residents of Nevada, although they might change their minds six weeks later, after obtaining a divorce. Mr. Drackert said that practically all the other guests were women, but after looking me over he added that he didn't think they'd make enough of a run at me to keep me from working. Most of them had children to wrangle, he explained; a ranch was an ideal place to run children, who, if kept in Reno, might become addicted to faro or bingo. Out by the lake, I could commune with nature and get a lot of work done. There were dude horses, if I cared to ride—which I didn't—and if I wanted to swim, there was a pool as well as the lake. There was also a bar, but no wheel. The last point was the clincher. I told him I would be out the next afternoon, which would give me twenty-four hours to collect my thoughts and possessions. The Paiute Indians, whom I had not yet met, have a notion that you should take five days to make up your mind about anything, and although life doesn't often allow you that much leeway, I agree with the principle.

Once we had struck a bargain, Drackert began telling me some of the disadvantages of dude wrangling. One was the daily *corvée* of bringing a detail of the women in to shop and have their hair done, which accounted for his presence in Reno. All the women didn't come in every day, of course. The ones who wanted to go to town signed up on the previous evening. He would load eight or ten head in a station wagon, he said, and take off in the morning in plenty of time to get them to Reno before lunch, but if he made even a trivial detour of twenty or twenty-five miles to buy alfalfa or look over a quarter-horse colt, they would complain. "If they would only show some interest in what I'm doing, they'd be interested," he said. "But they're so blasé you can't do nothing for them." Arriving at the Riverside, which was the general rendezvous for dude-ranch people, he would turn the women loose unhobbled, and they would scatter on varied and mysterious missions, having been instructed to return at four-thirty, which they interpreted as five-forty-five. That would leave Harry with time on his hands, even though he had to load laundry or provisions for the ranch, or perhaps go over to the Washoe County Courthouse and testify that a guest had not left the State of Nevada overnight since signing his register. (Swearing falsely—with special regard to one's residence—is among the most serious crimes in the Nevada code. If it became prevalent, the hotel and dude-ranch industry would collapse. It carries a penalty of up to fourteen years in prison, and when the culprit gets out he has to start his six weeks all over again if he still wants a divorce.) While waiting for the women to reassemble, Harry would swap notes with other dude bosses and horses with other horsemen, and would also absorb all the unpublished local news, which in the height of the season is often fascinating.

At first encounter, the Drackert face appeared a bit severe and ministerial for a cowboy. Spectacles and tufted eyebrows gave him a slightly owlish look head-on; his profile rather favored the hawkbill turtle's; his complexion was rare-beef red and the line of his mouth determined. He wore a flat-crowned Stetson, a candy-striped shirt, and a miniature green four-in-hand tie—nothing flashy—above the regulation Levi's and cowboy boots. He was not big, but his shoulders and forearms were. "My old mother, in Pony, can never get used to me being in this business," he said a trifle sadly, in a clipped, farmerish accent, for he comes from Montana, where the buckaroos don't drawl. "She likes Herefords, but she says even sheep would be better than this."

Nobody mentioned Indians during my talk with Drackert, and it wasn't until the next day that I learned that the lake was on a reservation, of which the ranch had once been a small part. Wallie Warren told me about it while he was driving me out there; he was a friend of Harry's and had some business at the ranch. I could have waited for the station wagon and ridden out with the shoppers, but I felt suddenly shy. It had occurred to me that I was in the position of a lone Turkish child entering an Armenian orphanage. I represented the enemy. The ranch, Warren said, comprised only about forty acres, and it had originally belonged to an old-timer named Sutcliffe, who had squatted down there before the reservation was firmly established, and therefore claimed to have a prior right. Sutcliffe had run a roadhouse that was popular with fishermen in the days of the big trout. (The Paiutes in those days sold fishing permits to outsiders and hired out as guides.) Eventually, the United States government had disputed Sutcliffe's claim and got a court decision against him, but he had been allowed to regularize his possession by paying a few thousand dollars into the Pyramid Lake Paiutes' tribal funds. Now Sutcliffe and the trout were gone.

Contemplating the perils of my immediate situation, I gave little thought to the Indians. I was determining that my entrance among those offended women should be as diffident as possible, with a minimum of brash verbiage, and one eye always on the nearest exit. This proved an error, for my fellow-boarders turned out to be a civil lot. They sensibly declined, however, to let my presence restrain them from talking about their husbands. These, I gathered, were an indecisive pack—petulant and helpless. Not one woman complained of having been brutalized. Each, according to her tale, had simply tired of being a nursemaid and protector. The repudiation of this role evidently entailed a certain sense of guilt. None of them could figure how the poor devil she had left was going to get along without her. One of the prettiest had made her husband promise to call her at ten every night—midnight in their home town in Michigan—so she could be sure he had done nothing reckless. "I couldn't sleep otherwise," she explained. "I said unless he would do it, I just wouldn't get the divorce. He's so weak. What would I do if he got drunk and ran over somebody?" The husband must have sincerely wanted the divorce, because he kept his promise. Another woman relented after five weeks and four days and went home to a spouse in upstate New York who had been having an affair with a secretary twenty years his junior. "I just can't let her take advantage of him," she announced before she departed on this errand of mercy.

Once I knew what was wanted, I tried to cultivate a decisive manner, but I had made my mistake at the outset and the first impression proved ineradicable. My cringing amiability reminded them of their husbands. At dinner the first evening, I heard a woman behind me say, "I can always tell their ages by the backs of their necks." I turtled my head between my shoulders and dined from a slight crouch from then on. Long before the arrival of the raspberry sherbet, I was looking forward to an escape to the bar, which was lodged in a detached one-story building out by the road running past the ranch. It was the only bar between Sparks, a suburb of Reno, thirty miles south, and Gerlach, ninety miles to the north, and it therefore got occasional non-resident trade. The bar, however, presented unanticipated difficulties of its own. I have never been reluctant to buy a lady a drink, but there were thirty-eight ladies in residence at the ranch, and this offered a problem in economics. Nor was I sufficiently brazen to ask if they would reciprocate. On that first night at Pyramid Lake, I tried to ignore them by concentrating on a fixed point straight in front of me—a form of yoga I practice on buses when I do not wish to give up my seat. The fixed point was, naturally, behind the bar, and in order to hold it in focus, I had to keep ordering Scotches. After the fourth, I felt more at ease, and turned to look about me. At my right elbow was no fellow-boarder but an Indian, thick through the chest, wide in the shoulder, and wearing a gray uniform shirt like a New York state trooper's. Around his waist was a cartridge belt, from which hung a pair of handcuffs and a pistol in a holster, and he was drinking orange pop. He had a broad face, across which heavy eyebrows, long eyes, wide cheekbones, and mouth made four horizontal ridges. The nose was high but flattened across the bridge, the eyes heavy-lidded. It was a face from Aztec or Mayan sculpture, under a wide-brimmed hat. It wasn't until considerably later that I learned that the Paiutes speak a Uto-Aztecan language and are of the same stock as their co-linguals who drifted south into Mexico and founded an empire. The Paiutes stayed by their lake.

When I turned, the Indian put down his pop and said, "How do you like our pub?"

"Pretty nice," I said.

"It always reminds me of those pubs in London," he said.

"During the war?" I asked.

He nodded, and replied, "I was an M.P. sergeant."

"You a cop now?" I inquired politely.

"Indian police," he said.

"Have a drink?" I asked.

"No, thank you," he said. "I don't want to get Harry in trouble." He added, with a smile, "After four years bouncing those G.I. drunks around, I come home and it's still against the law to sell me a drink."

This was Martin Green. He told me that the reservation included the lake and a rim of land around it—narrow on the west shore, wider on the north and east. The Indians were all Paiutes, and they ran cattle on their range, just like the white ranchers.

"Not too many cattle," Martin said. "Maybe eighteen hundred head." I was to learn that "not too" is a favorite Paiute-ism in talking English. It seems to express a tribal fear of overstatement. Martin said he had been riding among the hills looking for strays; if an unusual number disappeared, it was bad for the reservation policeman. "They think I rustle them and sell them to Harry for beef," he said. The tribe ran its herd as a unit, but individual Paiutes owned individual beasts, which were distinguished by their owner's brands. The Indian livestock sometimes mixed with those of half a dozen bordering ranchers, and nobody on either side ever admitted to being able to find as many animals wearing his brand as he claimed he thought he had. "Not too trusting," the policeman said.

I said, not too originally, that he must find the reservation not too like the places he had been in with the Army. He said that it was not too, but that he kept in touch with the outside world by reading back-number magazines abandoned by the dude women. "I wouldn't mind too much to go back for a visit," he added. "But I prefer it here."

When I awoke next morning, I thought I could understand why Martin felt as he did. I saw the lake through the screen door of my room, cerule against the leonine mountains, with Frémont's pyramid standing out plain in front of me, and big birds I took for gulls like dots of cotton in the sky. They were actually white pelicans, which breed on an island in the lake called Anaho.

My first view of Harry's place, the previous afternoon, had rather dismayed me; it looked comfortable enough but hardly seemed the spot to cultivate detachment. The main house stood fairly close to the road, behind an old established lawn with flower beds and trees. (Vegetation of this sort is possible around Pyramid Lake only on land that has long been under irrigation; the stand of trees made the ranch a conspicuous landmark.) Behind the house were company streets of one-room cabins with porches, set around a swimming pool, and children of all ages, whom I took to be the unhappy offshoots of broken homes, careered whooping through all the interstices between the buildings. I knew the mothers would do nothing to increase the children's sense of insecurity during this tragic interlude in the little beasts' struggle toward adjustment, and there wasn't a chance that they would shut up of their own accord. I could picture myself seated on a hut porch typewriting with all the privacy of a street portrait artist at the Greenwich Village art festival. The mothers themselves looked all right—very all right, some of them, in shorts and halter things —but they would not be particularly conducive to concentration, either. Joan Drackert, Harry's wife and hostess, had saved the day by suggesting a room in a second ranch house, high up on the side of a hill. The approach to it was protected by a railroad embankment and a deep gully, which one crossed on a shaky plank. In front of this house was a big empty corral and, nearer, a green lawn with fruit trees around it, and I proposed to set up my typewriter on a table under one of them. There were no other guests in the house. I had made my way to it up the hill and across the plank with the aid of a flashlight, holding numerous jack rabbits and ground squirrels transfixed in its beam until I had passed.

This first morning, which announced itself hot, I decided on a swim in the lake before breakfast. I put on swimming trunks and sneakers and, taking along a towel and a pair of shorts, started out, but before descending from my hill I had a look around. On the upland side of the house there was a corral smaller than the one in front. Three saddle horses, with powerful forequarters and small heads, were eating some coarse hay that had been thrown down for them. They had thin necks and barrels, and showed no more signs of grooming than deer; there was something feral, too, in the nimble way they walked. A little stream coming down the slope in a gully skirted one corner of this corral and ducked out of sight behind the house. I could see a shack a couple of hundred feet up the gully, and while I was looking at it, three slender men came out, wearing wide hats and blue denim pants and jackets, and walked down to the corral, where they saddled the horses. They were all Indians, and as they rode up into the bare mountains above, it seemed to me that they sat the deerlike horses with a special grace—romanticism on my part, no doubt, because the Indians ride the same saddle and seat as other cowboys.

I followed the little stream down toward the railroad embankment. Watercress grew along its banks, which were shaded by cottonwoods. There was no point in its course at which a child couldn't step across it, but so scarce is water in that country that every rivulet has a name and is indicated on county maps. This was Hardscrabble Creek. There were big, *bel-canto* bullfrogs in it that drew more water than the channel provided, and once I met a rattlesnake there, though not that first morning. Rattlesnakes can live in arid country, but they apparently prefer to live elsewhere; at any rate, they are as grateful for shade as an Arab. The stream didn't run all the way to the lake; it sank away in a sump under the railroad embankment, up which I scrambled. On one side of the right of way stood a schoolhouse made from a boxcar painted yellow, with windows cut in it and a stovepipe coming out the roof; it had a flagpole and a privy, and captive wasps buzzed inside the locked windows, among dead, unwatered geraniums. Looking up the track to the north, I could see three or four other boxcar houses and a more ambitious genuine house, made of railroad ties and also painted yellow. It had a fence and a cottonwood tree, and it belonged, I learned later, to the section foreman. Beyond this house was a water tower. Directly across the track from the school stood a telegraph office, in another converted boxcar, with a sign on it reading "Sutcliffe," which, it turned out, was the name of the small community. The telegrapher was up and about. To judge by the smell of coffee, he kept house in the car. He had a long nose and wore a green eyeshade, a vest, sleeve bands, and a heavy gold watch chain and seals, like a copyreader on the old New York *Sun*. He waved to me and asked me in for coffee, but I was determined to have my swim and declined.

I had had no idea when I moved into the Pyramid Lake Guest Ranch that its environs were so populous, for this little settlement was invisible from the road. The railroad, I discovered during my stay, was a branch line of the Southern Pacific that carried no passengers. It ran clear up to Klamath Falls, in Oregon, and handled a good deal of oil, machinery, and sundries going north, and miles of lumber for California coming back. The trains were seldom less than a hundred cars long, and their locomotives, blow-ing through the night, compared vocally to those of other lines as the Hardscrabble bullfrogs compare to the effete batrachians of Eastern ponds. These trains seldom travelled by day, except when an automobile was approaching a railroad crossing, whereupon one of them would instantly arrive and block it, usually for at least half an hour. The smaller houses along the track belonged to the water tender and section hands. One of the latter was an Indian married to a Mexican woman, another a Mexican married to an Indian woman; the water tender, a Swede, wore a peaked green military cap, like a railroad official in Europe, and had a neat garden around his boxcar.

I crossed the tracks and passed down by the ranch's horse corrals, which contained nothing Harry was proud of, he had told me, except an old thoroughbred mare in foal to Suncap—a horse I had seen win at Belmont long before—and a three-year-old palomino stud Harry thought he could sell for a good price. The rest were just dude horses, not as good as the ones the Indians rode, which were fast and handy. The dude horses were safe and phlegmatic, and looked it. As I went through the gate into the ranch grounds, an elderly itinerant blacksmith was shoeing the palomino colt. It was the colt's first set of shoes; he hadn't been broken long. The smith had his forge and gear in a trailer, and Harry told me afterward that he had hit Pyramid Lake early that morning and was heading for jobs on ranches farther north. The old man had picked up the colt's near hind foot, and the colt was trying to walk around him, throwing him off balance. "You son of a bitch, I'll give you a good going over," the blacksmith was saying, in a firm, mild tone. "You goddam bastid, you're just like your old man." They were family friends.

Once I had issued from the ranch grounds and crossed the road, the character of the land changed. Here the puny Hardscrabble would have seemed a Nile. The ground was covered with rock shard and a scrubby bush called greasewood. Tiny lizards, their tails over their backs, darted between these plants with such velocity that I thought at first they were low-flying insects; it was as hard to isolate their motions as to perceive a hummingbird's wings. Then I reached dunes of sand, wind-ridged like dunes by the real sea, and found the timbers of a small pier, two-thirds buried. Somebody at some time must have kept a boat down by the lake, which was now otherwise naked of landing places. The relic made a fine towel rack.

I had walked perhaps a mile from my lodgings and had passed from mountainy foothills, through green slopes, lush flatlands, and desert, to a Dead Sea shore, strewn with broken bits of white tufa. I sat down on the timber, facing the water. Viewed in this way, on its own level, the lake looked oceanic. I sketchily remembered reading that in some past geological era practically the whole of what is now the Great Basin, from the Rockies to the Sierra Nevadas, had been covered by inland seas, and I had no doubt that the lake was a rock-lined pool that hadn't dried up. When I got my lips wet, the impression was confirmed; it tasted like faded sea water. Under the surface, the water was clean and cool. When I came up after swimming a few strokes underwater, I turned on my back and found I could float easily. I swam out about fifty yards, performing all the clumsy acrobatics I never do when under observation. Returning to the shore, just short of where the beach rose, I dived at something on the bottom and landed with a dead fish in my hand, a thing of prehistoric appearance, with a head like a sea robin's and a body like a young sturgeon's. It was a cui-ui, I learned when I got back to the ranch and described it to Harry. He said it must have died of some chasmic malady, for cui-ui never take a hook, and, except in the spawning season, remain in the depths. In the spawning season, the Indians catch them with spears, and sometimes with bare hands, and smoke the flesh for the winter. The annual run of cui-ui has diminished, but a fellow I met subsequently, who had done some diving in the lake with apparatus, said there were plenty fifty feet down; maybe they have invented a new system of breeding. I used the towel I had brought along, changed to my dry shorts, put on my sneakers, and walked back to breakfast, feeling as if I had enjoyed a plunge into the Mesozoic era. Indian cattle—good-looking Herefords—were drinking at the lakeside. They apparently like the flavor.

I have since discovered that my thinking about the origin of the lake was a bit oversimplified. It was indeed once part of Lake Lahontan, the lesser of two great inland seas that occupied much of the basin in the distant past. Lahontan covered forty-five thousand square miles in northern and western Nevada, southern Oregon, and eastern California—an area about the size of England. But Lahontan dried out almost completely, leaving behind a few pools, like Pyramid Lake, that dated back to the time of the siege of Troy.

When I got to the main house after my swim, only a few late risers were still at table. Fifteen women had gone off riding, and eight others, dressed for town, were fuming while Harry, out back, loaded a nervous mare into a horse trailer, which he was going to hitch to the station wagon. (He told me that evening he had dropped the mare off at a ranch where they had a quarter-horse stud.) I sat down at a table with a pair of women and ordered a couple of soft-boiled eggs. The waitress, a Finnish war bride, was working her way to a divorce. She was very pretty, but she said her husband's parents in Fresno hadn't liked her. One of the women at the table had a grown-up son in Connecticut. She was telling the other about the concern she had felt for him on his wedding day. "I wasn't sure he had done right," she said.

"Well, you couldn't be with him, of course," the other woman said sympathetically. A fairly lush brunette, she was grazing forty. Her trouble, it seemed, was that her husband hadn't wanted his grown children to know he had remarried. "He wanted them to think we were living in sin," she said. "He was afraid that if they knew, they would raise hell about his will. It took all the satisfaction out of the penthouse. It was humiliating."

I remarked that this was a new twist.

"He's crazy," she said. "They'll poison him."

"Not if he sticks to soft-boiled eggs and opens them himself," I replied, looking mine over carefully as they arrived.

Before heading up the hill to my ranch house, I paused in front of the bookshelves in the living room to see what I might have to fall back on for amusement when the Scheherazades ran out of stories. Because my mind was on Indians, I picked out a paper-covered volume bearing the title "Program of the Carson Indian Agency, Jurisdiction Nevada-California—1944." There was nothing else in the Indian line, so I took it along with me, primarily, I suppose, to have an excuse for not immediately getting down to work. Arriving at the house on the hill, I lugged my typewriter and papers outdoors, placed them on a table under an apple tree, and began to read the Indian report, which had been issued at the Indian agency at Stewart, near Carson City. The first section was headed "General Information About the Carson Jurisdiction." The Carson jurisdiction, I knew, takes in the Pyramid Lake Paiutes. Under the subheading "Cultural and Economic Conditions and Standard of Living," I read:

> The Indians of this jurisdiction do not have the traditions and religious customs that are so evident on many other reservations. The early missionary influence is not particularly noticeable. The traditional Indian dances and Indian costumes are conspicuously absent. . . . Nearly every reservation has an annual festival which takes the form of a rodeo. Gambling is common and participated in by both men and women. The State of Nevada is notorious for its gambling, and it is therefore not surprising that gambling is so prevalent among the Indians. [The author might have added, in fairness to all, that the Indians were gamblers before there was a State of Nevada. They are gambling Indians.] Only a few of the older Indians are unable to speak English. The reservations are small, which places the Indians in close and frequent contact with their Caucasian neighbors. The majority of the men have worked for ranchers, in mines, or for the railroads and have proven themselves capable and acceptable. Some ranchers prefer Indian help to handle their livestock. Since the beginning of the war, many have secured and are holding good positions in defense plants.

The author was exercised because some of the Indians, having learned that they could earn three and a half days' pay by working Saturday and Sunday, were working only those two days each week.

Despite the opportunities afforded the Indians, the author noted regretfully, "the standard of living is still far from satisfactory. . . . The average family income for the jurisdiction is about $700." The average for the Pyramid Lake Reservation, I observed in an appended table, was considerably higher—$856. The average Pyramid Lake family, according to this table, received $17 in tribal rights (such as a share of the money received for leased grazing privileges), $15 from "irrigated agriculture," $157 from livestock, $539 from wagework, $37 from arts and crafts (gloves, moccasins, and beadwork), and $91 in relief and social security. Out of this average income, the average family paid an average of $50.85 on loans to the tribe from the United States government for the purchase of livestock. I knew, of course, that the average family is nonexistent, and that some Paiutes must be better off than others. Still, I didn't think there would be any spectacular economic spread on the reservation. Some figures on cattle ownership, a bit further on, confirmed my suspicion. They showed that sixty-six Pyramid Lake Paiute families owned livestock. Of these, the top three owned more than seventy-five but fewer than a hundred head each. The largest group—twenty-six families—owned from ten to nineteen animals each. Only one family owned as many as ten horses. Fifty-six families owned no livestock, and therefore had no resources but labor, relief, or servicemen's allotments. Nowhere in the list of incomes could I find signs of the government largess that Indians are popularly thought to receive. Whatever the Paiutes got, apparently, they worked for.

Of the origin of the reservation, I read:

On December 8, 1859, the Commissioner of the General Land Office, with the approval of the Secretary of the Interior, directed the surveyor at Salt Lake City, Utah, to set aside and reserve the Pyramid Lake Reservation, at that time unsurveyed, for the use of the Paiute Tribe of Indians who were living there. In 1865, Eugene Monroe, pursuant to instructions from the Indian Office, dated April 20, 1864, surveyed the outer boundaries of the reservation. On March 23, 1874, President Grant issued an Executive order reserving the Pyramid Lake Reservation as surveyed by Eugene Monroe.

The outer boundaries of the reservation comprise about 475,162 acres. The General Land Office survey of 1911 shows a land area of 313,772.14 acres. The recession of the lake, since the survey, has increased the land area considerably. [The area exposed by the receding lake was classified as "beach sand and of little agricultural value."] The land is owned by the Pyramid Lake Paiute Tribe, incorporated under Section 16, Act of June 18, 1934 (48 Stat. 984) as amended by the Act of June 15, 1935.

The Indian population of the Pyramid Lake Reservation consists of 598 individuals. . . . Of the total, 455 are full blood, 87 are ¾ but less than full blood, 47 half but less than ¾, and 9 less than half but more than ¼. . . .

The elevation of the reservation ranges from 3,820 at Pyramid Lake to about 8,100 feet above sea level near the north end of the reservation. . . . The maximum and minimum temperatures recorded at Nixon [the village near the mouth of the Truckee] are 107 degrees above and 24 degrees below zero, Fahrenheit, respectively. . . . The topography in general is uneven, and a large part of the reservation is characterized by rugged, rocky mountains. . . . All of the agricultural land is on the river bottoms. . . . The mountains are steep and rugged, with only a thin mantle of rock debris or soil on their slopes. . . . The soils are fertile and productive when properly irrigated. . . . There are 528 acres of cultivated crops on 936 acres of subjugated and irrigable land. [This meant that hardly one acre in five hundred of all this beauty would grow potatoes.]

All land on the reservation is in tribal status. The Indians do not lease any land to or from non-Indians. The Tribal Council has assigned the irrigated land to individuals. The 68 assignments vary in size from 1.4 acres to 30 acres, with an average of 11 acres. . . . The assignees are unable to make a living on this small area and abandon the land to seek more gainful occupation elsewhere.

The range lands [as distinguished from the crop-growing lands] consist of approximately 339,000 acres. Most of the usable range land lies between 4,000 and 5,000 feet above sea level. About 15 per cent of the land area has no grazing value and an additional 79 per cent requires more than six surface acres per animal unit month. [This meant that six acres of such land would not be enough to carry one beast for one month.] The carrying capacity of the reservation is estimated to be 23,000 animal unit months. [This meant that the range could carry rather less than two thousand beasts, if put to maximum use.]

What the Pyramid Lake Indians principally needed, the author wrote, was more irrigable land, on which to raise hay to carry their herd through the winter. There was one hopeful note: "Through court action, an addition of approximately 630 acres of irrigable land (Wadsworth squatter land) has been repossessed." Wadsworth is a town inside the southern tip of the reservation. I read on:

The timber resources of the reservation are relatively un-important. . . . An estimated 74,000 juniper fence posts and 5,500 cords of cottonwood occur on the reservation. The cottonwood trees constitute the main source of the fuel supply. No oil or gas is known to be on the reservation. . . . No deposits of important minerals are known at the present time.

The Indians hunt rabbits, quail, and occasional deer on the reservation. The amount of game secured on the reservation does not constitute an important part in their economy. In the past, fishing constituted an important source of food and also a considerable cash income. The lowering of the lake level, its increasing salinity, and the silt being brought down by the river are the main causes of the greatly decreased fish population. Fishing is relatively unimportant as a source of food and is of no importance as a cash income.

Three successive allusions to the "squatter land" at Wadsworth confused me. The first, as I have noted, cheerfully asserted that it "has been repossessed." The next stated, a bit less firmly but still optimistically, that "with the recovery through court action of approximately 600 acres of irrigable agricultural land the land situation will be somewhat relieved." Not "has been relieved," however. The third read, "The eventual recovery of the 'squatter land' at Wadsworth will help but not solve the problem." So it evidently had not been repossessed, after all. But I assumed the matter had been settled in the five years that had elapsed since the report was issued.

Turning to my own work, I found that from where I sat I could look across the corral to the lake and to the beautiful, niggardly mountains that wouldn't support cattle. The drop of the hill hid Sutcliffe and the ranch, but the tops of the telegraph poles along the railroad line reached into my field of vision. I sighted at the lake through the crotch of a cottonwood, using the top of a telegraph pole as a bead, and laboriously began to sketch. I lined up a triangle of water in the crotch, and, above it, a segment of mountain looking like a head-on view of a loaf of sandwich bread. By the time I had covered six sheets of paper with sketches, it was time to go down the hill again for lunch.

My experience with Indian warfare dates back to a version of the Battle of the Little Big Horn that was fought in the original Madison Square Garden in 1910 by the members of Buffalo Bill's Wild West Show and Congress of Rough Riders of the World. This began, as I remember it, with an unprovoked attack upon a stagecoach by half the Indians in the show. General Custer and his men, in blue uniforms and big hats, temporarily retrieved the situation, but the assailants, reinforced by the other half of the Indians, returned and rode concentric circles around his brave band, exploding blank cartridges and war whoops until they did him in. Then, as they howled and danced in fiendish aboriginal glee, more United States Cavalry dashed out on the tanbark and overwhelmed the Indians with blank-cartridge firepower, sabring the survivors, whose riderless ponies dashed for the stables in the basement. I eagerly awaited the arrival of a third batch of Indians, who would cut up the soldiers, who, in turn, would be avenged by another set of bluecoats; it was a plot susceptible of endless pleasurable repetition. But that part of the entertainment was ended. The United States Cavalry had triumphed until the next performance, and I felt sure the Indians would never be allowed to win.

This faith was shaken that day at the ranch, when I got down to the main house and found two armed Indians squatting on the lawn and stroking with visible covetousness the blond scalps of a pair of the children of broken homes. The bar, where I paused for a drink before lunch, was in the possession of three more Paiutes, who were sitting at a table and playing a curious game of poker, as noisy as the usual varieties are silent. They had side bets up for high and low card of every suit in the deck, and they collapsed with laughter at the end of every hand. Each of the Paiutes had a revolver strapped to his belt and a Winchester big-game rifle leaning at his elbow, and although they had not yet offered violence to the dude women, it was evident that they were in control and could take over whenever they wanted. Joan Drackert, who was behind the bar, calmed me. There was a Chicago woman staying at the ranch, she said, whose Reno lawyers had heard that her husband, in the best Chicago tradition, had employed some torpedoes to kidnap their two children, who were with the mother. Consequently, the woman's lawyers had retained Martin Green to provide a bodyguard, and Martin had deputized all the otherwise unemployed members of the tribe to act as guards, for five dollars a day—the going wage for buckaroos—plus bologna sandwiches and pop. The three Indians at the table were wearing expert-rifleman badges from the Marine Corps. "It happens a couple of times every season, and it always turns out to be just a rumor," Joan said. "But the Indians enjoy it, and it gives the place atmosphere."

That evening, or a couple of evenings later, I asked Harry the story about the squatter lands. He said it wasn't much. The way he had heard it was that a dozen or so old fellows like Sutcliffe had settled on Indian land in the early days of the reservation. The Indians didn't appear to care about the land as long as they had a lake full of fish; they used to take wagonloads of those big trout to Sparks and Reno and sell them in the streets there. But the government began getting fussy along about the time of the First World War, and set a price on each and every squatter ranch inside the reservation. After the court had denied Sutcliffe's claim to his ranch and he had paid up, most of the other squatters paid up, too, especially those on the west side of the lake. But some of those down at Wadsworth, on the southern end of the reservation, didn't. These were Italians, descendants of the early agricultural settlers of Nevada, the majority of whom came from the north of Italy to California in Gold Rush times and moved on into Nevada in the eighteen-sixties, to raise truck and fodder for the miners in mushroom towns like Virginia City and Austin. When the old Central Pacific Railroad built its shops at Wadsworth, some of the Italians went along, and started farming there to supply the workers. After the shops moved away, in 1905, they and their families stayed on and became ranchers. But they never paid for the land, except a first payment. Later, when the fish population of the lake declined, the Indians said they wanted the land back, and in 1936 the government started eviction proceedings against the squatters. Pat McCarran had brought in a bill at every session of Congress since 1937 to give the squatters the land or let them buy it at depression prices, but the Indian Bureau had fought it, and he had never got it through. "The squatters took their case to keep from being evicted to the United States District Court and win," Harry said, "but the guvmint appealed it to the Circuit Court and win there. But then the guvmint couldn't get a United States marshal here to serve the dispossess papers. They was all appointed through Pat. Now the Indians say they're going down and fence the lands back into the reservation themselves. There's a lot of hard feelings."

I said it was a hell of a thing when a government couldn't enforce its own decisions, but Harry said there were two sides to the matter. After all, those squatter families had gone and cleared that land, and raised children on it, and the Indians wouldn't do anything with it if they had it; they just thought they would. "An Indian don't want to work any more than he has to," Harry said. "Why, they had a boy over to Nixon could punch harder than any welterweight I ever saw, but he wanted to stay amateur—no ambition. He said if he turned pro, he'd have to train for long fights. 'Anybody I can't knock out inside three rounds I ain't interested in fighting,' he said. That's how they all are."

"That's got nothing to do with their right to the land," I argued. "Why, good Lord, Harry, you might say some millionaire is fooling away his money and you could make better use of it. That doesn't entitle you to take it away from him."

"I don't know about that," said Harry. He knows several divorced millionaires.

"Why, that's Communism, Harry," I said, thinking this would be the clincher. "You've got to be for property rights, even if it's an Indian."

"You know what old Pat says?" said Harry. "He says an Indian ain't *got* no goddam rights." Then he added hastily, "But he's an arrogant old cuss. And I don't hold with him."

"Well, if he's against property rights, he's a crypto-Marxist-Saint Simoniac," I said.

"I never heard that about the old goat," Harry said. "But he grew up on a ranch on the Truckee himself—he's still got it—and he says an Indian won't work except for wages."

Harry went on to tell me that there were two factions in the tribe—one, made up of old Indians, that wanted to wait and see what the government would do for them, and one that wanted to take the land immediately. The head of the action party, Avery Winnemucca, claimed descent from Winnemucca, the chief who led the Indians at the Battle of Pyramid Lake, in 1860; in that battle the Paiutes brassed off enough tinhorn gamblers and fake-mining-stock promoters to fit out a set of Bret Harte. Harry said there wouldn't be any shooting this time. "You see, those Indians and those ranchers are neighbors," he explained. "They all know each other since they was kids, and when an Indian gets into trouble over to Fallon or Fernley, and gets thrown in the jail, he sends for old Bill Ceresola, the head squatter, to come and bail him out. And Bill does."

When I discussed the subject with Martin Green, he assured me that recovering the land might make a good deal of difference to the Indians. The previous winter had been a hard one in Nevada, he said, and a lot of the stock out on the range had been winterkilled. "That land may not sound too much," he said. "Only about two thousand acres, and only six or seven hundred irrigated. But it would just increase the good land we have by about one hundred per cent. If we'd had that extra hay, we could have carried a lot more cows over."

It would be inaccurate to say that I found the dispute over the squatter lands a major interest during my stay; if I had, I'm sure I would have inquired into it further at the time. (As it happens, the only Amerindians I'd ever had ten words with before that summer were a Cherokee strip-teaser—from the Cherokee Strip, I suppose—and a Mohawk prizefighter, both of whom I had met in my reportorial youth.) But without further inquiry, I became convinced that the Indians were being cheated, because all the Indians I had ever heard of had been. The urban American's consciousness of the Indian is like Isaac's of Ishmael—tinged with mild guilt. Every New York school child learns that the island of Manhattan was bought from the Indians by the Dutch for twenty-four dollars in trade goods, and a sense of guilt over this cheating still persists, even though we present residents of New York didn't cheat them—nor, in most instances, was it our own personal ancestors who cheated them. The place names on Long Island and in Westchester recall those Indians: Quogue and Speonk and Chappaqua, Katonah and Amagansett and Montauk—everywhere you turn there is a reminder of the injustice that was done to them, an injustice of a remote, irreparable, and therefore comfortable variety.

I had my work to do and, moreover, I became, like most people in the same legal circumstances, a calendar watcher. The routine was an easy one to fall into. There was the daily swim in the solution of cold boric acid, the walk back across the hot sands, the two daily struggles with prose and somnolence under the apple tree, and, in the evening, the bar and such characters as Loco Jack Denton, who was the proprietor of a gold mine in Wild Horse Canyon, north of the reservation—an old gentleman with a fully furred face, like a Bedlington terrier's, whose only tipple was straight vodka. "I used to eat the glasses, but now I give 'em back," I heard him tell one of the divorce girls. This Loco Jack spent eleven months of each year up in his canyon (whether he got any gold out of it was a moot question—he liked to be mysterious—but he always had the price of a drink), and the other month he would make merry in Gerlach, which is a one-minute stop on the Western Pacific.

Among my fellow-guests was a small, serious woman named Penelope, who spent her internment dutifully reading the Existentialists in French and preaching the gospel of permissive child culture. She had with her a daughter, named, I think, Lorena, whom she allowed to set so poisonous an example for the other children that their mothers talked hopefully of Lorena's chances of foundering herself with Coca-Cola. When this changeling was momentarily short of original ideas for torturing her mother, she would throw herself on her back and lie there screaming until Penelope set her right side up. Penelope wouldn't take a drink; her life with Lorena was like a long operation without an anesthetic. On the day of Penelope's graduation at the Washoe County Courthouse, however, her lawyer, a traditionalist, insisted on buying her a champagne cocktail to toast the happy future. She liked it, and by the time she reached the ranch for her farewell dinner, she was an emancipated woman. She had had a couple more, and she was not a bad-looking woman at all, which nobody had noticed before. In the bar before dinner, she got a lock on old Loco Jack with her left arm and let him buy her a Moscow Mule. Then she told him a story about her husband that made that old coyote change color under his whiskers—the pink sifted through in a sort of orange-belton effect.

Penelope was just setting down her second Mule when this dreadful Lorena, who had been fed with the rest of the young stock before the adult sitting, drifted into the bar. She was feeling particularly mean, because she hadn't seen her mother since noon; it was the longest Penelope had been away from her during their whole stay. Lorena ran up behind her dam, threw herself backward flat on the floor, and instantaneously turned her face the color of a blue plum—a trick she could perform at will. She let out a scream like an ambulance in a traffic jam and kicked her heels against the floor until shavings flew. Penelope let her lie there until Peggy Marsh, the barmaid, had made her another drink, and then she turned around and said, "Get up, you little bum." Lorena clammed up instantly and got to her feet. Her mother said, "Now get the hell out of here and go to bed." Lorena turned around and ran like a high-tailed lizard. "She's just like her old man," Penelope told us all.

Still, I was sufficiently interested in the Indians to go over with Joan one day to the Paiute village at Nixon, in the delta of the Truckee, and take a look around. Indians are very social people; the Pyramid Lake Paiutes have several hundred thousand acres of homesites to choose from, but they all live in Nixon, or within a few miles of it. The north end of their cattle range is nearly fifty miles away. On the road between Sutcliffe and Nixon, skirting the shore of the lake, there is just one tree—a cottonwood, on the land side, about halfway along. But when you get to Nixon the scene becomes pastoral—like a Constable or a Morland. There are great, feathery trees, both cottonwoods and willows, along the river and the irrigation ditches, and bands of dairy cattle in the fields. The landscape is soft, the foreground taking the sting out of the mountains in the distance. Two state highways, one following the lower part of the west shore of the lake and the other the east, converge at Nixon and continue as one road down to Wadsworth, where they join United States Highway 40. At the crossroads in Nixon there are two general stores—the post trader's and Abe & Sue's—and near them an Episcopal church, a rectory, a barnlike gymnasium, a school, and a house for the teachers (there were then three in residence), all in a kind of general American rural style. Spreading out from this center are groups of houses, varying from square one-room shacks, like the ones children construct of playing cards, to the sort of buildings you see from a train going through the dingier suburbs of Chicago.

The yards were full of fat cats and lean dogs, and children who were also lean. (The only explanation I could think of for the difference in *embonpoint* was that the cats might be good at catching field mice and ground squirrels.) I went into a couple of cabins with Joan, who was placing orders for deerskin gloves and moccasins to sell in a shop she had set up at the ranch. There wasn't much in them except iron beds (four or five in a room, sometimes), stoves, kitchen chairs, utensils for cooking, and old magazines—nothing specifically Indian. They reminded me of the interiors of Arab houses at Thélepte, a village in Tunisia, where the iron bed and the sewing machine were the most indigenous objects on view. The Paiutes have had no tradition to follow in house furnishing, of course; before Frémont's time, and for a long time thereafter, they lived in rock caves or in brush shelters built over shallow excavations. Their women can still make the withe baskets and the corded robes of jack-rabbit skin that they used then, but these things are now far too valuable to use; they can be sold for the price of a lot of Woolworth household ware. Dented automobiles stood in the yards of most of the houses; around one man's house there were so many, all driverless, that I asked an Indian we talked to if there was a crap game inside, or a convention. He said it was simply that man's custom; he bought the cheapest cars he could find, never paying more than twenty-five dollars for them, and when they gave out, he left them in the yard, since it wasn't worth while hauling them away. "He likes the looks of them, too," my informant said. "Gets lots of laughs."

Abe Abraham, the Indian who ran Abe & Sue's, was unique—a Paiute full of business zeal. His store was air-conditioned; he called it the air-conditioned tepee. (Paiutes have never had tepees.) He stocked everything from popsicles to horse harness, including a full line of frozen foods and paper-covered books. Sue, his wife, ran a lunch counter in the store. Abe was tall and brisk, Sue short, stout, and just as brisk. Abe had been born on the reservation, and had worked as a plasterer in Reno until he got enough money to start the store, in competition with the old post store, which was operated by a white trader. "The trouble with these Indians is they don't want to learn a trade, work, get ahead in life," Abe said, sounding like a white Nevadan. "You work in town, you got to cut the mustard. You can't cut it, out you go." Abe showed me some bottles of mucuslike jelly and said they were specimens proving the existence of oil on the reservation—an Indian dream ever since the Osages down in Oklahoma struck it rich. Abe had books on mineralogy, which he insisted I look at. He was in correspondence with half a dozen oil companies. He told me that McCarran had passed the word around that if the Paiutes would let his friends have the disputed acres, he would get a two-million-dollar federal appropriation for a housing project at the gypsum mines in Empire, seventy miles to the north, and then all the Indians could get constructions jobs on it and make a lot of money. "It was no go," Abe told me. "We didn't want jobs anyway." He said the big hitch in the land fight now was that the only irrigation ditches across the repossessed land had been built by the squatters, who claimed the Indians had no right to use them. The land wasn't worth anything without water on it. The squatters' argument seemed suspect to me, since I had always figured that when you owned land you owned the use of everything on it.

As I have said, however, the Indians were not among my principal preoccupations that summer, and I came back home without going any deeper into the long wrangle. I had to stay out there about a week longer than Penelope. On the morning after her revolt, she woke up with a hangover and remorse and went back East with her devilkin and remarried Lorena's father. It was a terrible indictment of sobriety.

Old Winnemucca, an important nineteenth-century leader of the Northern Paiutes. (Courtesy of Nevada Historical Society)

Sarah Winnemucca, daughter of Old Winnemucca, lecturer, and author of *Life Among the Piutes,* 1883. (Courtesy of Nevada Historical Society)

Alida C. Bowler, Nevada Indian Agency Superintendent and defender of Pyramid Lake Paiutes, who is standing by one of the original boundary markers at the Pyramid Lake Reservation. (Lucile Hamner Collection, courtesy of Nevada State Museum)

Nevada Senator Patrick McCarran, who worked to legalize the taking of Indian lands. (Courtesy of Nevada Historical Society)

Derby Dam, which in 1905 diverted roughly half the annual flow of the Truckee River from Pyramid Lake. (Courtesy of Special Collections Department, University of Nevada, Reno Library)

Avery Winnemucca with Lahonton cutthroat trout. (Courtesy of Becky J. Smith)

Ted James. (Reprinted from a periodical published by the Bureau of Indian Affairs, *Indians at Work,* vol. 7, no. 12, and vol. 8, no. 1 [Aug.–Sept. 1940]: 14)

Martin Greene, military policeman. (Courtesy of Flora Greene)

Levi Frazier Sr. at the Fallon Rodeo. (Courtesy of Churchill County Museum and Archives)

Warren Tobey on Pyramid Lake. (Courtesy of Carmen Tobey)

Katie Frazier, tribal elder and the subject of an award-winning film, cleaning cui-ui on the lakeshore. (Margaret Wheat Collection, courtesy of Special Collections Department, University of Nevada, Reno Library)

Cui-ui and Indian fishing gear. (Gus Bundy Collection, courtesy of Special Collections Department, University of Nevada, Reno Library)

Paiutes fishing for cui-ui at the delta of the Truckee River. (Gus Bundy Collection, courtesy of Special Collections Department, University of Nevada, Reno Library)

Paiutes fishing for cui-ui at the delta of the Truckee River. (Gus Bundy Collection, courtesy of Special Collections Department, University of Nevada, Reno Library)

2

Some species of fish never take a bait the first time it is presented. They nibble, go away, decide they must have more, come back, and strike. In putting together the pieces of a complicated situation, I follow a similar pattern of behavior. While I was idling away a good part of the summer of 1949 by the shores of Pyramid Lake, in Nevada, I learned that the Paiute Indians on the reservation that surrounds the lake were engaged in a long contest with several families of white ranchers over the use of some two thousand acres of land, of which about six hundred were "under the ditch"—that is, irrigated, or at least irrigable. In that vast, generally arid country, irrigable land has a value hard to imagine here, for it can produce the alfalfa necessary to carry cattle over the brief winter. Without this supplementary feed, the sparse, enormous range is all but useless. Both Indians and whites are cattlemen in the Pyramid Lake country; riding the range, they look precisely the same. The whites' original "predecessors in interest," to employ a legal term with which, since my first trip out there, I have become very familiar, squatted on the disputed land at about the time of the Civil War, and the Indians have been trying intermittently ever since to get them and their descendants off. Some Indian Commissioners—there have been twenty-seven since the argument started—have made honest efforts to aid the Paiutes. Others have abetted the squatters. In 1924, Congress passed a bill allowing the squatters to acquire legal title to the land by buying it at an arbitrarily fixed price. By 1936, they hadn't paid up, and the Department of the Interior, of which the Bureau of Indian Affairs is a part, called the deal off and undertook to evict them. The Indians had never consented to the proposed sale, but up to that time nobody had asked them.

As soon as the Department of the Interior, then headed by Harold Ickes, asked for possession of the land, the late United States Senator Pat McCarran began introducing bills to give it—or, at worst, sell it for practically nothing—to the squatters, who according to him weren't squatters at all but the unfortunate successors in interest to stalwart pre-reservation pioneers. He contended that the reservation hadn't been founded until 1874. The Indian Bureau said 1859, according to its interpretation of the facts. The predecessors arrived in the interval between those two years. By 1949, when I arrived at Pyramid Lake, McCarran had introduced seven of these bills, one into each new Congress. Five of them had passed the Senate; none had got through the House.

Meanwhile, the government, acting for the Indians, had carried the eviction case through the United States Circuit Court of Appeals and won, and the Supreme Court had refused to hear a further appeal. But with McCarran still vigorous at sixty-eight and as full of bills as a cui-ui fish is of eggs in spawning time, the settlers wouldn't give up. The cui-ui, or *Chasmistes cujus,* is a fish found nowhere in the world but in Pyramid Lake—it has relatives in certain lakes in Utah, Oregon, and India—and the early Paiutes who lived around the lake were known to their neighboring tribesmen as "cui-ui eaters." McCarran was equally *sui generis* and equally indigenous to Nevada. In 1949, as a sideline to his Indian-fighting, he was trying to get a loan of a billion and a half dollars for Chiang Kai-shek, who was in the process of being chased out of China, and one of fifty million for General Franco, and, in addition, was raising hell with the Maritime Commission, the Civil Aeronautics Board, the United Nations, and the idea of European aid for anybody *but* Franco. While McCarran continued to introduce bills for the squatters, each side out in Nevada found a way to make the disputed land useless to its opponent— the Indians by fencing it into the reservation, and the ranchers by cutting off the water from its irrigation ditches. The ranchers said the water rights didn't go with the land; to obtain them would entail a whole new litigation. Without water, the land was drying out, and Indian cattle were dying on the range in winter for lack of the hay the deadlocked acres might have produced.

I listened with interest to a good deal of talk about these matters while I was out in Nevada, but when I got back to New York, Pyramid Lake seemed very far away from the view out of my favorite window at home, which includes the North River piers where the great Cunarders and Frenchmen lie. By Christmas Eve, 1952, however, McCarran was with me again. I could see the lights on the Liberté, once the Nazi Europa, as she lay at her berth with two hundred and seventy-one of her seamen still on board because they had snubbed the brand-new McCarran–Walter Immigration and Nationality Law by standing "on their rights as free men not to reply to questions"—a quotation ascribed by the *Times* to a delegate of the French seamen's deck union. If the sailors had been willing to answer the questions, they would have been welcome ashore, even though they had been Nazis or members of the Fascist Milice in France during the war. It was a measure of the extent to which McCarran had been able to force his opinions on his brother palefaces. On Christmas morning, the *Times* carried a picture of Senator McCarran himself, returning from a South American cruise on the Santa Rosa. He was sitting at an immigration officer's elbow while the officer interrogated members of the Santa Rosa's crew. Roman-nosed and full-jowled, the Senator had his white hair combed out in a laurel-wreath effect. He looked like the Emperor Galba on a coin—a guaranteed-by-the-government ninety-and-a-half-cent-an-ounce silver coin it would have to be, of course, since McCarran, in collaboration with other Western senators, had forced the United States to buy a billion and twenty-five million dollars' worth of silver in the world market during the years between 1934 and 1942, in order to maintain the price of domestic silver, of which the total production amounted to a bit over three hundred and forty-seven million dollars' worth. I wondered whether McCarran, while on his cruise, had thought of a way to have the Paiutes deported. To find out if he had, I telephoned to a neutral white I know named Harry Drackert, who runs a guest ranch at Pyramid Lake, and asked him how things stood between the Indians and the Italians. (All the squatters are of Italian descent—a fact that has its political bearing on the case.) Harry said that nothing had changed. The Indians still had the waterless land and the squatters the landless water. Pat had introduced one of his bills to take the land in the 1951 Congress, and it had bogged down as usual. But it was a cinch he would introduce another come spring, Harry said. "I entered for the state legislature myself, and I would of run good if I could of broke in," he added, passing to other news of northern Washoe County. "The only trouble was I got stuck in the gate. I was beat out in the primary."

"Wouldn't the Indians vote for you?" I asked.

"This was a Republican primary," Harry said. "All the Indians is registered Democrats. I got beat by one vote—twenty-one to twenty. If Joan could of voted for me, I'd of tied." Joan is his wife.

"Why couldn't she vote for you?" I asked.

"Turned out she's a registered Democrat, too," Harry said. "If I'd got nominated, I could of won, because all those Indians would of voted for me instead of the Democrat in the elections. As it was, the Democrat won easy. The pay would of helped buy penicillin for those yearlings I got. Come New Year's, they'll be some of the runningest two-year-olds in America."

"Quarter horses?" I asked. In 1949, Harry, who used to be a world's champion rodeo rider, had owned mostly dude horses, but had aspired to better things.

"These is thoroughbreds," Harry said. "I got a stud—Andy K. —and I'm using him on my mares."

I shuddered. Andy K., I remembered from seeing him race at Saratoga, was an extremely fast horse with an incurable habit of running out on the turns.

"Do they run—" I began, but delicacy prevented me from completing my question.

"I don't know," Harry shouted, understanding. "I ain't got them up that fast yet."

I cannot deny that curiosity about Harry's two-year-olds increased my desire to revisit Pyramid Lake. So did an effectively simplified version of the situation that I had built up in my mind during the intervening months, which went like this: Here were these funny Indians, the first I had ever known and, unlike my preconceptions, neither solemn nor tragic nor mysterious but dressed in J. C. Penney cowboy clothes and talking, like everybody else in that part of Nevada, about the two annual staple crops of the region—Herefords and divorcées. I had heard all sorts of yarns about what the narrators called Indian shiftlessness. For example, there was one that hinged on the disappearance of the great cutthroat trout from the receding lake. When the level of the lake dropped, the cutthroat had found it impossible to ascend the Truckee River, the lake's lone feeder, in the spawning season. The reasons for the drop were two—a cycle of dry years, beginning in 1917, and the diversion of water from the river for a power plant and irrigation ditches along its course. After the trout had disappeared, the State Fish and Game Commission offered to restock the lake with a species that would not have to go upstream to spawn, on condition that when the new trout caught on, other residents of the state would be allowed to fish for them, provided they bought a tribal license. The Indians, according to the story, turned the Commission down cold. They wanted the lake for themselves. I had also heard that they would not permit prospectors on the reservation—although, for all anybody knew, it might be shot full of valuable ores—because they just didn't want to be disturbed. This lack of a soaring, General Motors type of ambition appeared to be a hereditary characteristic. "The old Paiutes never had anything but a pot to cook in, and even that was only a watertight basket," an Indian Bureau man had told me. "They'd cook in it by filling it with water and heating the water with hot stones. They'd take the pot and wander after food—berries, or small game, or grasshoppers, or pine nuts—always using the lake as the center of their orbit and counting on the fish for their main supply. They were unpretentious Indians."

The unpretentious Indians, however, were standing off the internationally omnipotent old calliope of a Senator. I had never met McCarran, but I had heard a miscellaneous lot about him, and in the months that followed my talk with Harry I pursued a lazy kind of research on the subject of the Senator. I looked in the Congressional Directory and saw that he was born in 1876—in Reno, it said, although I had been given to understand he was born on a ranch a few miles out, which he still owned. He had four daughters, two of whom were nuns, and a son. He had taken his A.B. at the University of Nevada in 1901 and been admitted to the bar in 1905, dates that showed him to have been about four years older at both stages than the average candidate. While studying law, he had farmed and been a member of the state legislature. It must have been a tough grind, and I could imagine young McCarran, only a few miles from Pyramid Lake, envying his Indian contemporaries when they took off to go fishing. There is nobody so resentful as the man who wants to get ahead; instead of being grateful to other people for not competing with him, he wants them to be miserable, too. The Senator's parents, named in the Directory as Patrick and Margaret (Shea) McCarran, had, I knew, been Irish immigrants; the elder Pat had gone to Nevada as a soldier in the Regular Army in the sixties. For Nevada, that's Mayflower stock; out there, you can't go more than ten years further back without being a Washoe or a Paiute. The Senator had "practiced in Tonopah and Goldfield during the mining boom of those places," the Directory said; he had been District Attorney of Nye County, which includes Tonopah, from 1907 to 1909, and had then "resumed practice in Reno." He had been Associate Justice and then Chief Justice of the Supreme Court of Nevada between 1913 and 1918, as well as state chairman of the Four-Minute Men, who sold Liberty Bonds in movie theatres during the First World War.

After again resuming private practice, in 1919, he had been president of the State Bar Association in 1920–21, although, I knew from reading elsewhere, in 1920 there had been talk of disbarring him because of an instantaneous divorce he obtained for Mary Pickford by exploiting a loophole in the law that concerned the state's residence requirement for divorce, which then was six months. According to this neglected aperture in the statute, if the defendant in a divorce case could be served within the same county of the State of Nevada in which the plaintiff resided, he might be haled into court and a decree granted instantly. Miss Pickford's husband at that time, Owen Moore, wandered fortuitously into Douglas County (pop. 1,400), where his wife just as fortuitously happened to be. A McCarran catchpole, apprised of the astonishing coincidence, served his summons. Mr. Moore appeared in court in Minden, the Douglas County seat, and the

Douglas County judge forthwith severed the knot, accepting the assurance of both parties that there had been no collusion. McCarran had not discovered this loophole; a lawyer named Sheldon, the father of the Nevada divorce business, had for some time been working it for obscure clients and relatively inconsequential fees, being reluctant to publicize the goose that laid small but regular nuggets. McCarran's resort to it left Miss Pickford free to return to Hollywood and marry Douglas Fairbanks, which she did (in a wedding of international interest), with no interruption of her professional career as America's Sweetheart. She turned over to McCarran a house in Reno, which he still owned at the time of his death. Its acquisition in the first place had been part of the tactical screen with which he masked his strategic intention; the house indicated that Miss Pickford meant to stay the full six months. After her return to Hollywood, she had no use for the house, so McCarran took it in trade.

The explosion of indignation that followed Miss Pickford's divorce showed how strongly Nevadans resented a threat to a basic industry. The Governor of Nevada and the local Bar Association and Chambers of Commerce denounced the outrage, which, if made a precedent, would permit bipedal sources of income to escape from the state without running up a board bill. Sheldon was indicted, but the indictment was dismissed; he had not written the law. That set a precedent, so McCarran wasn't indicted at all. There was newspaper talk of annulling Miss Pickford's decree, but that would have delegalized the status of Miss Pickford and Mr. Fairbanks, and the faith of America's younger generation might have been shaken forever. In the end, the Governor and the legislature decided to let bygones be bygones, and simply amended the statutes to plug up the loophole. This made Sheldon so mad that he went to Hollywood and became a movie producer.

Musing upon this *Märchen* of old Nevada, I resumed my scrutiny of McCarran's skeletonized autobiography in the Congressional Directory. (The Senator had omitted any specific reference to the Pickford case, even though it marked his first emergence as a name in the national press. On that occasion, he had shot across the firmament like a meteor, and had then gone out like a three-dollar-and-forty-nine-cent Fourth of July flowerpot.) The entries covering the next dozen years were sparse; the Senator noted that he had been president of the Truckee River Water Users' Association in 1921–22, vice-president of the American Bar Association in 1922–23, and chairman of the State Board of Bar Examiners in 1931–32.

As the depression began to take hold in Nevada, the legislature, by way of countermeasures, lowered the residence requirement for divorce to six weeks and relegalized gambling. (Games of chance had been banned in 1910 by an over-optimistic legislature that thought the gold mines would hold out.) McCarran, for all his lifetime of striving, was hard up; he might as well have gone fishing with the Indians all along. In 1932, all but six of the banks in Nevada closed. Of the collapsed ones, all but three were owned by another Goldfield and Tonopah man named George Wingfield. The depression levelled a lot of scores. Up to that time, Wingfield had had all the luck that had evaded McCarran. He had gone into Nevada as a cowboy driving cattle down from Oregon to provide ten-dollar steaks for the gold-rushers. He had worked as a bartender, then had traded a stickpin for a claim, which he ran up into an empire with full Congressional representation in Washington. A square-shouldered old man with hard, tight fists, he had won fortunes in poker by pretending to be dull. The stables he built for his racing stud are now a deluxe motel. Wingfield did things in style.

McCarran found a way out of his difficulties. He got himself elected United States senator. To do this, he had to beat Tasker L. Oddie, a Nevada bipartisan institution. The primary function of a senator from Nevada is to get all he can for the home folks. In order to get it, he needs leverage, and he attains this by seniority. Unlike Southern states, which can attain seniority only within the Democratic Party, Nevada can accumulate it in both parties—in the Senate, that is. It won't work in the House, because the state is entitled to only one congressman. Oddie was the Republican and Key Pittman the Democratic member of a team aimed at the big double; both men were popular in the state and, since they never had to run against each other, they could always pretty much count on re-election. If 1932 had been a normal election year, the system would have made Oddie a hard man to beat and the Democrats would have had trouble finding a candidate willing to have his throat cut. But McCarran recognized how abnormal 1932 was. He volunteered for nomination. His posters read, "A New Deal for America: Roosevelt, Garner, and McCarran." When he was elected, he at once began bucking Roosevelt and Pittman to prove his independence.

A second Democratic senator from Nevada made Pittman feel like a high-school senior with a new baby sister. Pittman, then sixty, was only four years older than McCarran, but he had been a United States senator since 1912. He had mined in the Yukon and then lawyered at Tonopah, where he and McCarran had been rivals in high-flown frontier hyperbole. The senior Senator from Nevada, who was chairman of the Senate Committee on Foreign Relations, was a red-hot anti-dictator man, and called isolationism "that damn word." Along with Oddie's place in the Senate, the newcomer took over his moral obligation to the squatters—in 1924, Oddie had got the bill passed that let them buy the land. Besides, the squatters themselves were McCarran's fellow-members of the Truckee River Water Users' Association. So it was an important test for him when he went to bat for his first Pyramid Lake bill, on April 12, 1937, before the Senate Committee on Indian Affairs.

There is to my taste no better reading than the straight record of a good hearing or trial. Accordingly, in order to follow the junior Senator's maneuverings, I wrote to the Government Printing Office for all the available printed records of the hearings on the McCarran Pyramid Lake bills, of which there were now eight —s.840, 92, 13, 24, 22, 30, 17, and 2, in the Seventy-fifth, Seventy-sixth, Seventy-seventh, Seventy-eighth, Seventy-ninth, Eightieth, Eighty-first, and Eighty-second Congresses, respectively. Luckily, I suppose, I received the records of only three hearings—substantial little paper-bound books of about a hundred and fifty pages of small print each. Hearings on the other bills either had not been printed or were out of print. The works supplied were dated 1937, 1943, and 1949, relating to bills s.840, 24, and 17, respectively, and provided a well-spaced selection chronologically. I was especially pleased that the 1937 hearing was included, for I could thus be present as McCarran made his initial sortie. I felt that I was seeing the curtain rise upon a play I had already heard a good deal about when I read the title on the cover of the 1937 volume:

FIRST SESSION ON S.840
A bill to authorize the Secretary of the Interior to issue patents for certain lands to certain settlers in the Pyramid Lake Indian Reservation, Nevada.
April 12, 13, May 3 and 17, 1937

The names of the fourteen members of the committee appeared on the inside cover. (Of the fourteen, only one has survived into the present Congress—Senator Dennis Chavez, of New Mexico.) But only four attended the hearing of April 12, 1937, which was held in Room 424-A of the Senate Office Building. Chavez was one. The three others were Elmer Thomas, of Oklahoma, chairman; Burton K. Wheeler, of Montana; and Lynn Frazier, of North Dakota. "Present also" were Senator McCarran, of Nevada; John Collier, Commissioner of Indian Affairs; James M. Stewart, Chief, Land Division, Office (later the Bureau) of Indian Affairs; and J. R. T. Reeves, Chief Counsel, Office of Indian Affairs.

The hearing opened quietly enough, like one of those plays that begin when a butler walks out on the stage and answers the telephone.

THE CHAIRMAN: We have before us for consideration this morning s.840, a bill introduced by Senator McCarran: "Be it enacted by the Senate and House of Representatives of the United States of America in Congress assembled, That the

Secretary of the Interior is authorized and directed to issue to each person who entered lands under authorization of section 1 of the Act entitled 'An Act for the relief of settlers and townsite occupants of certain lands in the Pyramid Lake Indian Reservation, Nevada,' approved June 7, 1924, or to the successor in interest of such person, a patent for the lands so entered for which part of the purchase price has been paid, without requiring that any further sum be paid on the principal of such purchase price or the interest on the unpaid part of such principal."

The chairman then remarked that the Department of the Interior had made an adverse report on the bill and, upon being asked by Senator Frazier, "What is their objection?," read a letter signed by Charles West, Acting Secretary of the Interior, who wrote, among other things:

At the time of the filing, one-fourth of the purchase price was paid, the balance to be paid in installments with interest at five per cent. None of the five entrymen [squatters] who would be affected by s.840 made any further payments. . . . Claims of the entrymen that the appraisals were too high were considered, and on November 30, 1934, the appraisements on their entries were materially reduced. The interest also was reduced from 5 per cent to 4 per cent. No interest has been paid by any of the five entrymen. [The five entrymen were J. A. Ceresola, W. J. Ceresola, Domenico Ceresola, M. P. De Paoli, and a number of Garaventas incorporated under the name of the Garaventa Land & Livestock Co.]

The proceedings continued:

SENATOR WHEELER: How did they originally file on an Indian reservation?
SENATOR MCCARRAN: May I make a statement?
THE CHAIRMAN: Yes.

And we were off.

SENATOR MCCARRAN: Mr. Chairman, the history of this
runs into the history of Nevada. In 1864, the Central Pacific,
now the Southern Pacific, was constructed through Nevada.
At that time, certain settlers came in on the Truckee River at a
point that was established as a division point by the Central
Pacific Railroad, known as the town of Wadsworth, located
on the Truckee River about 35 miles east of the city of Reno,
and about 15 or 16 miles from Lake Pyramid.

In 1859, an order was made by the Interior Department
that a survey be made of certain territory surrounding Pyramid Lake with the idea of thereafter creating an Indian reservation for the Paiute Indians. Nothing was done about that
order, or anything subsequent to that order, until 1874. [Ac-
tually, I found, a lot of relevant things happened during that
period.] These dates are significant, and I would ask you to
bear them in mind as I go along. Along about 1864, as I have
stated, settlers came in on the Truckee River close to the town
of Wadsworth, and there took up arid lands, constructed a
ditch, and diverted water from the river and irrigated the
lands. . . . There was then no reservation, nor was there more
in contemplation of a reservation than what I have stated;
namely, a letter saying that a survey should be later made and
that it should be set aside for the Indians.

These settlers took up tracts of land and cultivated the
land, irrigated the land, and established farms thereon. . . .
The successors of those early settlers are now in possession,
and have been at all times. Many of them are families or descendants of the early first settlers. [As a matter of fact, none
of them were. The first settlers were roughnecks with German and Irish names.] In 1874, President Grant issued an executive order creating an Indian reservation and ordered that
a final survey be made establishing the lines of the reservation. I draw your attention to the difference in dates between
1864, 1865, and 1866, when the early settlers went in there, and

the date of the executive order by President Grant creating the reservation.

SENATOR WHEELER: Of course, all over the West, when they filed on land prior to its being surveyed, they got a right, after it became surveyed, to take up those lands. [I imagine that he had had to fix up a lot of shaky claims for constituents, too.]
SENATOR MCCARRAN: Excepting in a case of this kind, Senator, where they had already been in, and then were surveyed into the reservation.

McCarran then expounded something that I knew to be true—that the "predecessors in interest" had been allowed to claim some land within the reservation in the sixties and acquire it in "fee simple," which, in lay English, means outright. They purchased it from the state at a dollar and a quarter an acre. "So that if the government should eject these five entrymen from the tracts of land in question they would not and could not eject the entrymen from the reservation, because they hold lands in fee simple adjacent to these very lands in question," McCarran said. What happened in the case of the fee-simple land was that the federal government told the infant Nevada state government in 1864 that it could have seven million acres of public lands, anywhere on the public domain, and could sell them to homesteaders. The money so raised was to be used for schools. In making the gift, the federal government did not except from the public domain the brand-new Indian reservation. Each of the five squatters' first predecessors on the Pyramid Lake Reservation had filed on one quarter-section—a hundred and sixty acres—and had then appropriated without formality several hundred acres of adjoining land. The argument was over only the acres that the predecessors had informally glommed onto. These, in the course of years, had become confounded with the original, legitimately acquired quarter-sections, and Reno banks had granted mortgages on land that included fee-simple acres along with the rest. It was as complicated as the history of Trieste, and Chairman Thomas's attention was evidently wandering.

THE CHAIRMAN: Are these Indians unable to make any further payments?

SENATOR MCCARRAN: They are not Indians; they are white settlers. Everything that I am saying here is set out in a letter from the Land Office, of which I have a carbon copy, dated Dec. 19, 1929. The copy that I have is unsigned, but it is on the official stationery, and the original is somewhere. I do not know where it is. I shall be glad to have someone look that up.

Everything I am going to say here is set out in the report of Senator Curtis as to Senate Bill 225. The report was filed Oct. 20, 1921. It is set out in a letter addressed to Senator Curtis and signed by E. C. Finney, Acting Secretary at that time. This gives a very interesting history of the whole transaction. It is more in detail than I shall burden the patience of this committee with, and it is so authentic, so emphatic, and so clear that I beseech your careful attention to it.

These references to the 1921 and 1929 letters turned out to be the first bars of a motif McCarran kept introducing at approximately the same point every time he played the tune. Finney, to whom he referred with the reverence usually reserved for somebody like Thomas Jefferson, served under Albert B. Fall, who was the bagman's dream of a Secretary of the Interior. The passage in the Finney letter that particularly appealed to McCarran begins: "As to the equities in the matter, originally these Indians were nomadic, obtaining their living chiefly by hunting and fishing. Essentially they were not agriculturists and knew nothing of the art of irrigation. . . . As to the lands immediately here in controversy, the equities in favor of the Indians are far from strong." The 1929 letter reads, in part: "The Indians have never been in the controversy and accordingly have done nothing toward the development of such lands. The white settlers have converted this wilderness waste into a productive and prosperous community." Neither letter mentions the fact that much of the manual labor on the lands in question was actually done by Indians, working as hired men on acres to which, the courts have since decided, they had much better title than their employers.

But back to the hearing:

SENATOR MCCARRAN: Let me continue. Nothing was done with reference to ejecting these settlers or doing anything about them until 1909. Keep in mind the dates 1864, 1874, and 1909.

SENATOR WHEELER: When did [the courts] make the appropriation of the water on these lands? Was it prior to the lands being an Indian reservation?

SENATOR MCCARRAN: Yes, sir. . . . Let me recite a little history to you.

The United States Government sought to adjudicate the claims of the Indians and the claims of the white settlers along the Truckee River. . . . The Federal Court, at the behest of the Government, did [issue a] decree, and that water is today a decreed [property of] these white settlers. What is more than that, under the law of Nevada and under the law generally, that water, being appropriated water, can be divested from the lands and sold by the white settlers, even though the Government were to come in and oust these white settlers. . . . [The Indians] would have nothing then but the bare land, valueless in that arid region. . . . To make this story a little shorter, this matter has been going the rounds between the Department and Congress and the courts now since 1864, we may say, and especially since 1924, when these settlers did pay up the part required of them at that time but were unable, and have been unable, to pay up since.

I have a very personal knowledge of the conditions of these settlers because I was born and reared in this very community. The very waters that irrigate the farm on which I was reared are the waters of the Truckee River, that also irrigates the farms of these men who were my neighbors during my boyhood days. I know their conditions. I speak of them and for them, because, if there ever were those deserving the consideration of Congress at this time, it is these five families which now remain there. They are honest, God-fearing citizens. . . . Here is a group of five unfortunate farmers who come before Congress now and say that by reason of financial conditions over which they have no control they have been unable to carry out their agreement. We only ask now that they be permitted to have the lands on which their families have been reared, on which they have married and given in marriage, and on which they have buried their dead, if you please. . . . They have been the sustenance of the Indians of that reservation.

Again I refer you to the letter of the Commissioner and to the letter of the Department in which it is stated that these Indians are not inclined to be agriculturists. . . . They are fishermen. They are nomadic. [They had occupied the same lands for several thousand years. I would have liked to hear the Senator's definition of a permanent resident.] They are a rambling tribe. They never showed any inclination, in their native state, to be agriculturists. But, be that as it may, and assuming that they could be converted into agriculturists—and we hope they can—there are approximately 300,000 acres in the Pyramid Lake Indian Reservation. There are thousands of acres—I have not the figures, but there are thousands of acres yet available for cultivation.

THE CHAIRMAN: Are there other lands available for irrigation purposes on which the Indians might go if they wanted to?

SENATOR MCCARRAN: Yes, sir. . . . The shortage of water is a thing that is common. Whenever the Sierra Nevada range is not heavily covered with snow, the Truckee River does not run sufficient water, but the Federal Court, protecting the rights of the Indians, has put a water master on that river, and they get the first right to the water, ahead of any white settler, for the Indian lands that are cultivated in the Pyramid Lake Indian Reservation. [The water master's chief duty is to see that each landowner takes only the annual share of water allotted to him by court decree. He is a federal official, but his salary is paid out of a kitty levied on these proprietors.]

THE CHAIRMAN: The facts are, as I understand, that there is plenty of good land, as good as this, susceptible to irrigation, that the Indians might go on if they cared to farm it. [There wasn't, of course.] So they are not being deprived of their homes, as are the Indians in some reservations?

SENATOR MCCARRAN: No, sir.

SENATOR WHEELER: What does your bill propose?

SENATOR MCCARRAN: My bill proposes that a deed shall be issued by the Department of the Interior to the white settlers.

SENATOR WHEELER: Without any further payment?

SENATOR MCCARRAN: Without any further payment.

The statement of John Collier, Commissioner of Indian Affairs, was pallid in comparison with Senator McCarran's heavily rouged exposition.

MR. COLLIER: . . . There is one date which has been omitted. It is undoubtedly covered in these various documents. It has been pointed out that it was in 1859 that the General Land Office directed that the Surveyor General of Utah reserve this area for the Pyramid Lake Indian Reservation.

SENATOR WHEELER: When was that?

MR. COLLIER: That was in 1859. That was merely a direction by the General Land Office to the Surveyor General. But in 1861, according to our record information, the lands were withdrawn from sale and settlement as an Indian reservation.

SENATOR MCCARRAN: By whom, Mr. Collier?

MR. COLLIER: By the Land Office. That reservation was not created until 1874, but the lands were withdrawn, in contemplation of creating a reservation, in 1861, so that no entry could be effected after that date. . . . No rights could have arisen after 1861 except through some act of Congress. There was no act of Congress until 1924. . . . Now, may I speak for a moment about the matter of the water, which is all-important in this country? . . . The water goes with the land. Is not that elementary?

SENATOR MCCARRAN: . . . No. . . . The courts of the West have decided it, Mr. Collier.

MR. COLLIER: . . . Leaving that question . . . if the Indians do not get this land, can they get the water to cultivate an equivalent amount of land?

SENATOR MCCARRAN: It has been decreed to them.

MR. COLLIER: But the water does not exist.

SENATOR MCCARRAN: May I answer that? Would you want information on that, Mr. Collier?

MR. COLLIER: Yes.

SENATOR MCCARRAN: If water does not exist, it is because nature does not produce it. [This statement, one of the profoundest dicta of a gigantic mind, has no rival that I can think of.]

SENATOR WHEELER: It seems to me that the question involved here is one similar to the one we have had upon other Indian reservations. First of all, there is no question at all that the equities are with the white people.

MR. COLLIER: That is one side. The other side is this, Senator. . . . From the standpoint of the Indians' position, the situation is simply this: They have not got, at present, at least, the irrigated land on which they can make a living. They are developing the cattle business and they need this land to supplement it. . . . If it were put up to the Indians whether they would take back the land or the appraised value, they would take the land today. . . . The Indians want this land.

SENATOR WHEELER: So do the white people, and the equities are with the white people.

When I had read that far, I could see that the Paiutes had fallen into an ambush.

In the ensuing sessions of the hearing, Collier struggled gallantly, but in vain. I learned why the Indian Bureau had no authoritative witness on hand when I read:

MR. COLLIER: . . . I should like to be allowed to offer for the record a document that I do not ask the privilege of reading, because I do not want to take your time. It is the statement

that the superintendent, Miss Alida C. Bowler, superintendent of the Carson Agency, would have made had she been
able to testify. I would like to offer it for the record if Senator
McCarran has no objection.

The jurisdiction of the Carson Indian Agency, I knew, included all the reservations in Nevada. The character of a woman
Indian agent struck me as offering an attractive role for somebody
like Rosalind Russell. I had never before heard of Miss Bowler.
But McCarran apparently had.

SENATOR MCCARRAN: I want to say, Mr. Chairman, that ordinarily I would not object to this; and I do not care to raise
an atmosphere here that is not pleasant, but Miss Bowler's at-
titude in this whole matter has been so unpleasant; her published statements have been so unfair, and the fact that she
has resorted to unfair publicity in this matter, prompts me
in doing something that ordinarily I would not do at all. . . .
I understood the statement was made when we recessed . . .
that I did not want to face Miss Bowler, and that that was the
reason I withdrew. I wish that Miss Bowler were here. I want
to correct that statement. If she was here before, I am sorry
that I did not have the pleasure of meeting her. But the lady
has so reflected upon this committee, in the press and out of
the press, and has made it so much of a political issue, that I
must in the nature of things raise a question against any fugitive instrument that is not presented by the original author so
that cross-examination can be had. It is only in that spirit that
I raise any objection whatever; and if, after what I have said,
the chairman sees fit to admit it in the record, it will be all
right with me so far as I am concerned.

Abandoning Miss Bowler for the moment, Chavez and
McCarran now jumped all over Collier for giving pro-Indian
interviews to the press, to which Collier replied, "I do not believe
you will find anything to object to, except that you do not agree
with my views." The wrangle ended with the following passage:

SENATOR MCCARRAN: I do not think any of this is material. I only raised an objection in reference to this fugitive instrument. If she wants to present it, let her present it herself.

MR. COLLIER: She was here for weeks endeavoring to present it.

SENATOR MCCARRAN: I did not know that.

The letter was admitted to the record, but not until McCarran had launched out on a rhetorical, allegorical, pastoral-symphonical statement that outdid his exposition on the first day:

SENATOR MCCARRAN: I would like to draw a picture for this committee. It comes out of an expression that the Commissioner used, that the Indians want these lands; they do not want money, but they want these lands. It is not to be wondered at that they want these lands. These are highly cultivated alfalfa fields; beautifully cultivated alfalfa fields, indicating the everlasting diligence of man there, and in one instance the diligence of De Paoli, one of the entrymen. He has one of the nicest little ranches that you ever saw in your life. If this Congress were to permit this man to be ejected, here is the picture. De Paoli's house is over on his fee-simple lands. His barns and corrals are over on the disputed land. The line runs so that the home and hearthfire of his family, if you please, is on one side of a fence and his corrals are on the other side. The corrals are modernly constructed and are up to date.

SENATOR CHAVEZ: Probably other people would want the land, according to your description of it.

SENATOR MCCARRAN: Certainly. . . . This question involves the homes and hearthfires of these five poor, unfortunate families. And when I say they are poor, I say it emphatically, because for years I have lived by their side and I know what I am talking about. This whole question is one of fair play, justice, and equity. It is not one of cold-blooded, heartless law. We can oust these settlers; we can throw them out, and they will become destitute, unless perhaps their little holdings otherwise would help them to go on. Or we can let them live as they have lived for years and years, in neighborly friendliness with these Indians. . . . I know that there is many an Indian down on that reservation today that does not want those lands, but there is a group that has gone in there and has used political methods.

I say, without fear of contradiction, that today the superintendent of the Indians of Nevada is using the Indian vote as a political club to try to compel me to withdraw this bill. I do not fear any contradiction of that statement, because it is true. The Indians vote in Nevada, and their vote has been thrown in my face ever since I introduced this bill, and it can be thrown in my face just as long as I am in the Senate of the United States. But neither the Indian Bureau nor an imported Indian superintendent for Nevada can threaten me with any such club as that and get away with it. The time has gone by for cheap politics of that kind. [This was not quite so reckless as it sounded, because there are only five thousand Indians in Nevada, and three or four times that many citizens of Italian blood.]

I know the merits of this case, and that I cannot present it more forcefully is really a sorrow to me. These people came in there as early as 1864. [He meant, as usual, the predecessors, but he never missed a chance to promote this emotional confusion.] They came in in good faith on the open, public, unsurveyed domain of the United States. They have been continuously in occupation of those lands. They made what the Westerner looks upon as beautiful little self-supporting homes. They are in the desert country where no Indian ever grubbed brush before the brush was grubbed by these white people. No Indian ever constructed a ditch before a ditch was constructed by these white people. No Indian ever took possession of these lands in any way, form, or manner. So you are taking nothing whatever from the Indians. What they never had they never lost. . . .

McCarran then turned to the question of why the settlers had not made good on their payments for the land under the 1924 arrangement. "They could not get the money," he said. "I can testify under oath to this matter, to my personal knowledge of their efforts to raise this money. [At the time] you could not borrow a dollar on a twenty-dollar gold piece."

Miss Bowler, in her letter, wrote that the Pyramid Lake Tribal Council, knowing she was to be in Washington on other official business, had expected her to present their side of the case at the hearings. But the hearings had been postponed twice, and she had had to go back to her work in Nevada. "On September 17th [1936], the Secretary of the Interior requested the Attorney General to institute suit to evict these white squatters," she went on. "The Attorney General instructed the United States Attorney in Nevada to prepare the suits. But before he had filed these suits he received an order to bring no action until he received further notice. An exchange of wires revealed that this had been done at the request of Senator McCarran. . . . To date the suits have not been filed."

On May 3, 1937, I reëntered Room 424-A, Senate Office Building, via the transcript. Present, besides the chairman, were Senators Chavez, Frazier, and Frederick Steiwer, of Oregon. Wheeler was absent—possibly out fleecing some Blackfeet. Collier presented 1936 Washoe County tax records to prove that the settlers hadn't paid taxes on most of the land in dispute. He also offered data on the yield and prices of alfalfa in northern Nevada for the years when the settlers said they were broke. According to the figures, they shouldn't have been. Then McCarran arose and denied a story he said he understood was in Miss Bowler's letter, which he hadn't bothered to read. Informed that the story wasn't there, he said, very handsomely, "That is not my understanding. If you are correct in that, then I am in error, and I will be corrected." But as to Miss Bowler's personality, he remained bearish:

> SENATOR McCARRAN: The attitude of the lady who represents the department in the State of Nevada has been the most unfair that I have ever seen on the part of a Govern-

ment official. The result has been to arouse class hatred between races. [An amalgam of the evils of Marx *and* Hitler.] In
other words, the five entrymen here are Italians, and in every
publication that is made in the press of Nevada coming from
Miss Bowler, she refers to them as . . . "those Italians" or "the
Italians," drawing the line between the Indian population of
that particular section and the Italian population. [In his own
statements, McCarran had called them Italians, I remembered, and naturally he always called the Indians Indians.] . . .
So far as [the settlers] having any money is concerned, I give
my word of honor to this committee—and I regard that as
about the most valuable thing I have in this world—that no
such condition prevails.

On May 17, 1937, I returned once more to 424-A, by courtesy
of the Government Printing Office, to hear the closing discussion
of s.840. McCarran on this spring morning was all business.
He offered an amendment to his own bill, stipulating that the settlers, instead of getting the land gratis, must pay up in cash, but
"with the interest to date written off." Collier introduced what
I found a fascinating compilation of information on how the
"predecessors in interest" had done their squatting in the first
place. "One of these cases . . . is that of a white man who killed
an Indian in order to gain possession of the Indian's land," Collier reported, prompting the chairman to remark, "As far as I am
personally concerned, I have very little interest in that ancient
history."

The committee took McCarran's amended bill under consideration and eventually recommended its passage. On July 22, 1937,
it passed the Senate; in its final form it contained a provision requiring payments that totalled about twenty-two thousand dollars and one excusing the settlers from paying the interest that
had accrued since 1934. The House Committee on Indian Affairs
amended the measure to the extent of requiring, the settlers to
pay all the interest, and recommended its passage in this form.
But the Honorable James Scrugham, the lone congressman from

Nevada, organized an objection to the bill on the floor of the House, and it died there. Scrugham was a Democrat, too, and he detested McCarran just as heartily as McCarran detested Pittman. The House, jealous of its powers vis-à-vis the Senate, has a habit of following the wishes of a state's congressmen, rather than its senators.

A similar McCarran bill met the same fate in the Seventy-sixth Congress; so did another in the Seventy-seventh. By 1943, when McCarran dropped s.24 in the entry box, there had been a considerable change both in the Nevada Congressional delegation and in the state of the nation. McCarran was the senior Senator from Nevada, entering on his eleventh year of office. The obstructive Scrugham was his junior colleague, and a newcomer named Maurice J. Sullivan, a Democrat, was the Nevada representative. The change had been precipitated by the death of Senator Pittman in November, 1940, just after President Roosevelt's election to a third term, which McCarran opposed. "Nevada has lost an able and zealous representative and the nation has lost one of its greatest leaders," McCarran said at the time of Pittman's death. McCarran, however, had consistently refused to be led. During Pittman's chairmanship of the Committee on Foreign Relations, McCarran not only had never followed but had never even partially concurred. In February, 1940, he had voted against a loan of twenty million dollars to Finland for the purchase of arms, although the Finns had been attacked by the Union of Soviet Socialist Republics. Before Russia's involvement in the war against the Reich, he had gone down the line against compulsory military service, lend-lease aid to Britain, the dispatch of troops to Iceland, and the use of militia against strikers in a North American Aviation plant that was manufacturing warplanes. As a Party-line voting record on foreign affairs, McCarran's compared favorably with that of the late Vito Marcantonio. Pearl Harbor rather flabbergasted him, but six months after we entered the war he had found his own satisfactory *casus belli* against Germany. This came when eight trained Nazi saboteurs landed from submarines on the coast of the United States—four in New York and four in Florida. "If they landed—as they apparently did—in violation of the immigration laws, that is an overt act," McCarran said, and from then on he was as implacable in his opposition to the enemy as he had been in 1917, when he sold all those Liberty Bonds. From the benign, oleaginous first-termer who in 1937 had combined Western courtliness with Morton Downey charm in his entreaties for his original Pyramid Lake bill, he had changed, especially since Pittman's death, into a blustering, arbitrary type. But on May 20, 1943, when he descended into the House of Representatives, like Orpheus to plead for Eurydice, he reverted to his kindliest manner. His Eurydice was s.24.

The chairman of the House Committee on Indian Affairs was a Democrat named James F. O'Connor, of Montana, a cattleman in private life. "I might say that we had some hearings on this bill before," O'Connor began when McCarran's bill was put before the committee. "This is Senator McCarran's bill, and we will hear from the Senator first." And now, reading, I had the feeling of pleasurable anticipation that as a youngster I experienced once a year at the Palace Theatre, the capital of vaudeville, at Seventh Avenue and Forty-seventh Street, when the orchestra played a medley of "Ida" and "Roley-Boley Eyes," and Eddie Leonard, the great old minstrel man who never changed his act, made his annual appearance. During the intervening months, Leonard had been performing the same act at other theatres; by the time he got back to the Palace again, the audience was filled with a pleasant, because sure to be satisfied, nostalgia, as for turkey on Thanksgiving.

This time, the curtain rose on Senator McCarran saying, "A little of the history will do no harm, although it may be a little irksome on those who have heard me on this before. There is on the wall just back of you a map which portrays the locale of the land in question." This was an innovation since 1937. He had added props. But it changed nothing essential, any more than anything essential was changed when Leonard wore a new cinnamon-colored satin suit. Then McCarran read the passage from the anonymous report of 1929 about the settlers who "converted this wilderness waste into a productive and prosperous community." After that, he told how the railroad reached Western Nevada in

1864 and how the United States government gave the state seven million acres of public lands, which the state had allowed settlers to take up, and which accounted for the acres held by the squatters in fee simple, not to be confused with the land in dispute. The Senator was sticking by 1874, too: "In 1874, President Grant made an executive order in which he set apart lands surrounding Pyramid Lake, pictured on the right on the map, for an Indian reservation for the Paiute Indians. That was in 1874. Keep that date in mind. . . . It all hinges on the executive order of President Grant of 1874."

Now the Senator was back in 1860:

So along these rivers the white settlers took up the lands. . . . They took the lands at that time, and at the present we would perhaps call them "squatters." . . . They and their predecessors have been there and are now in occupancy of those lands continuously from the time they were first taken up until the present moment. . . . These white settlers are now ready to pay in full, plus the interest and all of the charges that have been made by reason of the appraisement of these lands, notwithstanding the fact, gentlemen, that the appraisal value is, in my judgment, far out of range of any land in that locality—$30 an acre for alfalfa land. Why, you can buy it for $15 an acre anywhere around there. They are willing to pay that high figure although their ancestors came in here as pioneers. They are the sons and daughters of pioneers. They were born on some of these tracts of land. Here they gave their young life, they were married, they gave in marriage, they buried their dead. [Like Eddie Leonard, he never cut a good line out of the act.] It has been their home from time immemorial for most until the present day . . . I will tell you why [the Indians] want these lands. [I could sense repugnance for their base motivation throbbing in his voice.] I will be frank. These lands have been cultivated for years and years. . . . They stand up like little green gems along the river. They do not require any hard work. There is no sagebrush there to grub. It has all been cleared and levelled, and it is pretty to look at, and it will produce crops right away if it has the water. . . . The settlers can move that water away from the lands if the land is taken from them so [the Indians] will have no ditch and no water. . . . Gentlemen, it is entirely a matter of equity and entirely a matter of justice. That is all that is in the bill.

A congressman named Fred Gilchrist, of Iowa, asked, "Well, has there ever been any decree against the [settlers] under which their rights were terminated?"

To this, Senator McCarran, with perhaps a trace of sorrow that anyone should ask him so pointed a question, replied, "The action commenced about a year and a half ago and was tried in the District Court of the district of Nevada, and judgment was rendered in their favor. That case was appealed to the Circuit Court of Appeals by the Government, and the judgment of the lower court was reversed. . . . That was against the white settlers. There is now an appeal on the part of these settlers to the Circuit Court of Appeals." This was not true. The Circuit Court of Appeals had rendered a verdict against four of the settlers, and had the fifth case still before it.

Mr. Gilchrist then ventured to say that thirty dollars an acre did not seem to him a high price for irrigated alfalfa land—especially during a war boom, when cattle were cash on the hoof, he might have added, but he respectfully refrained. McCarran said, "Thirty dollars is high, since we are remote from a hay market." [This was precisely one of the reasons the land was so valuable; if the Indians couldn't grow alfalfa for their cattle, they would have to send far and pay dear for it.] Gilchrist asked McCarran if he thought even President Grant in 1874 had a right to set up a reservation, and the Senator replied that personally he didn't.

Anthony J. Dimond, delegate from Alaska, confessed that he was still confused about the status of the lawsuit, and McCarran repeated that the district judge had ruled in favor of the settlers (he always began that way, like a Brooklyn fan who says that the Dodgers were ahead for eight innings, before admitting they lost), and then mentioned the regrettable action of the Circuit Court of Appeals. He referred the committee to the Finney letter of 1921, with its opinion that the equities were with the whites. (The strains of "Ida.")

Antonio M. Fernandez, of New Mexico—another state afflicted by uppity Indians—got the point. "Unless the Circuit Court is reversed, under its decision the Indians would have a legal title and could prevail in ousting the white settlers, unless something is done here," he said. Quite right, said McCarran. (He had done *his* best to prevent this shocking lapse on the part of our legal system, I have since learned. Immediately after the lower court's decision for the settlers, he had called on Ickes and asked him not to appeal it.)

Mr. Gilchrist, possibly being hungry, suggested adjournment, but Representative Sullivan, of Nevada, said he had two Indians from Pyramid Lake with him, "and they cannot stay very long because Washington is a very expensive place." John Murdock, of Arizona, said, "So we have found," and then, with all parties pleased by this exchange of Congressional jocosities, the committee resigned itself to hearing Sullivan and his savages:

MR. SULLIVAN: Mr. Chairman and gentlemen of the committee, I am sure you will agree that it is not a pleasant task for me to disagree with the distinguished Senator from Nevada. He has a duty to perform and he is doing it as he sees fit and I also have a duty to the people of my State and I trust the committee will give me credit for doing what I think is right and proper. . . . The present bill now before the Congress is an appeal from the court to the Congress. . . . These Indians are citizens and voters. More than 40 of their number are in the armed forces of the United States. This country is under a peculiar obligation to them by legislation as well as the most rudimentary principles of justice to treat them in good faith and to afford them at least equal protection under law. [The allusion to the Indians in service was the first reminder in the text that in 1943 the country was in the midst of a war.] The settlers who seek relief in this bill have paid an average of one-fourth of the purchase price of the lands and the appraised price has been reduced nearly 50 percent. Many of these settlers and their predecessors in interest have occupied the lands more than 50 years, and so long as title remained in the Government they escaped state taxation. The down payment does not even approximate a fair rental for the land or any return for the exemption from taxation so long enjoyed. . . .

MR. O'CONNOR: Now, under all of the circumstances, do you feel that these white settlers have any equities?

MR. SULLIVAN: I do not think so. I do not.

McCarran then went into his water-rights-explanation routine, disregarding the incredulity of Murdock, of Arizona, who interjected, "In my country, water rights go with the land and the two are inseparable," and after a bit more palaver, Sullivan introduced the Paiutes—Albert Mauwee, secretary of the Pyramid Lake Tribal Council, and Albert Aleck, the Council's chairman. Aleck, whom I know personally, spoke first, and I could visualize him before the Little White Stepfathers. A straight, slender, bespectacled man with thin, rather severe features, he supplements his income from a few head of cattle by driving the school bus on the reservation in winter. My feeling of inside knowledge was accentuated when I observed that the Government Printer had spelled Aleck's name wrong.

MR. ALEC [sic]: Mr. Chairman and gentlemen of the committee, this is the first opportunity we have had under the reorganization act to have a word in a matter like this. [The bill under consideration was the fourth of its kind to reach the Senate.] I will read our statement on it:

Need for land [Aleck read]: On the Pyramid Lake Reservation there is actually under irrigation 936 acres. Of this amount, 300 acres is an irrigated pasture down toward the lake which is very poor land, being sandy and subject to wind erosion and water erosion. . . . Of the 636 acres of irrigated farming land, 500 acres are in cultivation for crops and 136 acres are in irrigated farm pasture. This 636 acres is operated by 70 families. . . . On top of that there are 21 able-bodied heads of families living here right now who have no land at all. . . . It is our opinion that the average family should have at least 30 acres of irrigated land to be economically sound without any outside employment. . . . In 1942 the population of the Pyramid Lake Reservation was 288 males of all ages, and 278 females of all ages. . . . At the present time there are 37 men from Pyramid Lake in the armed forces. This is 12.85 per cent of the male population. . . . Nine of the 37 have volunteered, approximately one-fourth. None of these men have any land to come back to when the war is over. How are they going to make a living? . . . Why was the land reappraised in 1934? [Nobody else had bothered to ask McCarran that.] Is it customary when one party agrees to buy real estate from another party at a specified price to reappraise the property when the buyer fails to meet his payments? . . . We are free men. We are citizens of the United States with the right to vote, desiring to assume our full responsibility as citizens as fast as possible. . . . All we ask is justice, not as wards of the Government, but as free, self-respecting, patriotic Americans.

Some of the Western congressmen may have thought that another hand had written the speech for Aleck; in any event, they now began to put him through an agricultural quiz:

MR. MURDOCK: Did I understand from your statement that that land had been recently subjected to wind and water erosion of some sort so that it is not in very good condition? . . . Is that a recent happening?
MR. ALEC: No; it has been going on probably for as long as the weather.
MR. MURDOCK: You have a water right to a much larger amount of land, have you not?
MR. ALEC: Well, according to the record, but we only get the benefit of the water during the spring. In July and the last of the months of the summer, why, the water is cut down to very little. On the lower land, the sandy soil is such that we cannot very well keep up a crop under evaporation.

Then a number of the congressmen got into a powwow with the two Paiutes about agricultural details. It was friendly, for the most part, but all through it the congressmen appeared to assume that if the Indians could possibly get along without repossessing their lands, they ought to. O'Connor, the chairman, addressed the Paiutes as "you boys," but most of the other committee members were more civil. The chairman asked Aleck if his father and mother had been raised on the reservation.

MR. ALEC: Yes, Sir; to my knowledge they were. . . .

THE CHAIRMAN: Did you ever hear them say, or anybody say, as to who improved this land in the first instance?

MR. ALEC: Well, as far as my knowledge of it goes, why they have always sort of told us that they used to camp along that particular spot all along the river. At that time the Indians used to own quite a few horses all along the river bottoms and they used to build corrals for their horses and would camp at sites up and down the river from that point.

THE CHAIRMAN [apparently the kind of man who would keep on walking into a left jab]: That does not quite answer the question. Maybe I did not make it clear to you. It has been generally understood out there that the white settlers improved the land in the first instance.

MR. ALEC: Yes, sir; but there is one incident happened there. The Indians started ditching at one point, that is about the Ceresola place, and it can be seen a little today. I could not tell you for just exactly what reason they moved out of there. Some of the old Indian stories was that there was a party living below the Ceresola ranch and after the Indians went out fishing their houses were burned down. They were just made out of sticks and different other things and their houses were burned down and the women and children were killed. That is a story that I have had in my memory for quite a long time. . . .

A bit further on, Aleck remarked, "We are just a little minority group." This evidently needled the chairman, who demanded, "Where did you learn that expression, 'minority group'?"

"That is part of the modern vocabulary," Aleck replied.

Fernandez, making a last attempt to prove that the Paiutes didn't need their land, said, "You have got more water than you can use on the irrigated land."

Mauwee, a less frequent contributor to the dialogue than Aleck, said, "In July and August we cannot see it."

After that, the chairman blew the whistle, and the Indians were free to terminate their expensive stay in Washington.

The next day's hearing began with another item I had learned to expect—a statement by Collier. Collier, a bit stiff in his lines in 1937, had acquired confidence through familiarity with the script, and by now he played with almost as much authority as the star. He had a whole arsenal of court decisions and Attorney General's opinions, which he handled with a *maestria,* although not a *brio,* equal to McCarran's. To support the Bureau's contention that the reservation dated from 1859, not 1874, he went into what, when I was a high-school boy, we used to call a sequence of plays, in which, without waiting for signals from the quarterback, a team ran through a succession of maneuvers designed to annihilate the opposition psychologically as well as tactically. The steps in the formation of the reservation, Collier said, were, successively, recommendation by Special Indian Agent Major Frederick Dodge in a letter of Nov. 25, 1859; concurrence by the then Commissioner of Indian Affairs on Nov. 26, 1859; proclamation by the Commissioner of the General Land Office, with the approval of the Secretary of the Interior, on Dec. 8, 1859; posting of notices on the land in May, 1860; an attempt at enforcement by Territorial Governor James W. Nye in August, 1861 (the first squatters had already appeared); completion of a detailed survey in 1864–65; and, finally, President Grant's proclamation of 1874, which McCarran was still trying to palm off as the inception of the whole affair. According to Collier, it had been no more than a postscript to an epilogue. Collier went on to ring in the text of the decision of the United States Circuit Court of Appeals when, on July 6, 1942, it awarded the land to the Indians. In 1926, a United States federal court, he said, had granted the Indians water rights as of 1859, proving that the court must have recognized their land claim as of that year. Here McCarran, who in 1937 had made much of this decree, because it also gave the squatters water rights as of 1864, proving that they had been there before President Grant issued his executive order in 1874, appeared to shift his position. If the decree implied that the reservation dated from 1859, he naturally wanted no part of it. "The matter is still in a tentative form, being in a tentative decree; that is, being tried out by the water master under the direction of the federal courts for the time being." ("Tentative" was not quite the word. The decree was "operative" as of 1926; it was made final in 1944.)

Collier then went into his big speech, which showed a considerable improvement in style over his earlier efforts. "What we have here is a proposal to take property from one citizen for the benefit of another citizen; to take the property for private purposes," he said. "It is a taking in such a way that it probably would be unconstitutional as between white citizens or between citizens and Filipinos or between white citizens and Negroes, or between Negroes and Japanese. It is possible to do this thing to Indians only upon the theory that Congress can disregard constitutional restrictions in dealing with Indian parties."

The chairman said, "The Chair recognizes Senator McCarran," but Gilchrist interrupted him: "Mr. Chairman, I would like to tell the Senator and the Commissioner my point of view regarding this legislation or bill. I do not know which side it will help or hurt, but I am of the opinion that if there is litigation involving this very thing, then Congress ought not to step in and decide that lawsuit. If these parties are in court let them continue in court and have them take the results. I do not believe we should try lawsuits in the legislature."

McCarran, O'Connor, and Fernandez tried to talk Gilchrist out of such a picayune view of the function of the legislative branch of government. If Congress wasn't there to overrule the courts, they argued, what *was* it there for? McCarran began calling Gilchrist "Judge," which I took as an indication that he was worried.

Then there appeared in the text a name and, soon afterward, a prose style that have since become familiar to the nation. Karl

Mundt, a congressman from South Dakota at the time, spoke up. "What was the year when they were found in default?" he asked, explaining that he had missed the first day's hearings. In giving a brief synopsis of the case for Mundt's benefit, McCarran said that Secretary Ickes had been willing to accept his bill in 1938, after it had passed the Senate in amended form. "I would like to ask Mr. Collier the reason why Mr. Ickes has apparently changed his stand from then and now," Mundt said, and Collier told him that it was primarily because by now the courts had ruled clearly in favor of the Indians. "The property is Indian property without a cloud on it now," he said.

Another thought occurred to Mundt. "Is there anything peculiar about this deal which makes a difference between the parties?" he asked. "If a man buys a piece of land and makes an initial payment on it and then forfeits under his contract, he has no more claim than anyone else, has he?"

The bill died without coming to a vote in the House.

In December, 1943, the Circuit Court of Appeals decided the one remaining squatter case in favor of the government, and in 1944 the United States Supreme Court denied certiorari, which in nonlegal language means it declined to hear a further appeal. That would have stopped most fellows, but it didn't stop McCarran.

3

"The first outbreak of the American Indian in human literature," according to Mrs. Horace Mann, widow of the celebrated nineteenth-century educator, was achieved by a woman named Sarah Winnemucca Hopkins, who wrote a book called "Life Among the Piutes: Their Wrongs and Claims," published in 1883. Mrs. Mann's statement appears in an introduction she wrote to the book, and I found it hard to accept, until I tried to think of an earlier Amerindian author. I could recall only John Rollin Ridge, who was a son of a Cherokee chief and became a famous San Francisco journalist in the sixties. But Ridge was a half-breed who lived as a white man and wrote of nothing specifically Indian; his best-remembered book is a blood-and-thunder fictionalized biography of Joaquin Murieta, a Mexican bandit of the gold diggings. Mrs. Hopkins was a Piute, or, to go along with the orthography now approved by the Smithsonian Institution, a Paiute. Unlike the Cherokees and other originally Eastern tribes who had had contact with the whites for centuries before Mrs. Hopkins' time, the Paiutes had barely heard the English language when she broke out in it. Mrs. Mann certified that Mrs. Hopkins had no ghostwriter.

My own life among the Paiutes began in the summer of 1949, which I spent by the shores of Pyramid Lake, Nevada—the Paiute Mediterranean. It is a small Mediterranean, shaped like a pork chop and about thirty-one miles long, and the Paiutes are a small nation. They and their "predecessors in interest," to use the accepted legal tag, have occupied the littoral for some thirty-five hundred years. They are therefore as indigenous as jack rabbits. They do not, however, bore the stranger with genealogical anecdote. In this, they reminded me of William M. Stewart, the illustrious white Nevadan pioneer, who wrote in his autobiography, circa 1908, "I refrained from taking advantage of opportunities that existed to inform myself in regard to my ancestors, on account of the disgust I felt for persons of no consequence who were constantly boasting of their pedigrees."

At present, the Paiutes live on the Pyramid Lake Reservation, which surrounds the lake. The reservation has a land area of about three hundred thousand acres, of which only about nine hundred are fit to grow crops on. Lack of water is the problem, as it is in all of Nevada. On acquaintance with the Paiutes, I discovered that they had a cause, as well as an irredenta: some two thousand acres of land, including six hundred acres of good land—irrigated land—that had been misappropriated by white squatters ("pioneers" is the polite Western word) in the eighteen-sixties, and subsequently transferred to white successors in interest, who were still claiming it. A cause presupposes a history, and while retracing this dispute—its course winds like that of the Truckee River, on which the lands are situated—I came upon Sarah Winnemucca in the American-history room of the New York Public Library, whither I had trailed her through the card catalogue in the reference room. This was in 1953, shortly before I decided to revisit the lake.

Sarah was perhaps forty when she wrote her book, and she could remember the first encounter her maternal grandfather's band had had with white men. The meeting occurred at a big bend of the Truckee, near the lands that were to be so long in litigation; it is at this point that the river, which rises in Lake Tahoe and flows first north and then east, finally turns north again, to empty into Pyramid Lake. Sarah says in her book that "truckee" means "all right." It was her grandfather's name. The whites called him Captain Truckee and named the river after him, and the name stuck. I have read somewhere else that Truckee was not the old boy's Indian name but simply what the whites called him, because he was always saying "truckee." The whites thought it was a mispronunciation of "talkee." This is one more instance of the whites' egocentricity, as well as of their chronic underestimation of the Paiutes; the chief was saying "truckee" because he meant "all right," and he was pronouncing it perfectly.

Sarah remembered that the first whites she saw as a child

frightened her; she hid her face in her mother's apron of woven sagebrush fibre and wouldn't look again. They attracted her, too. "They had hair on their faces, and had white eyes, and looked beautiful," she wrote. The white eyes, of course, were actually gray or blue—pale by contrast with the black eyes of the Paiutes. Later, she overcame her fear. Captain Truckee and her father, Old Winnemucca, sent her to Johntown, an early mining camp, to board with the family of a Major Ormsby, one of the first settlers of Nevada, where she learned cultivated ways. Dan De Quille, the author of "The Big Bonanza," wrote, in 1876, "The people of Johntown, though not numerous, were jovial. Nearly every Saturday night a 'grand ball' was given at 'Dutch Nick's' saloon. As there were but three white women in the town, it was necessary, in order to 'make up the set,' to take in Miss Sarah Winnemucca, the 'Piute Princess' (daughter of Winnemucca, chief of all the Piutes). . . . When a Johntown 'hoss' balanced in front of the 'Princess,' he made no effort to economize shoe-leather." On page 12 of "The Big Bonanza," there is a picture of Sarah, a bosomy girl with hair falling to her shoulders. She is wearing a long-sleeved dress and lace collar. "When in towns and cities, she dresses after the fashion of American ladies," De Quille wrote, "but when with her people generally dons the Piute dress." As a young woman, Sarah became a versatile Pocahontas, serving as interpreter and mediator between her people and our frontier soldiers. In the course of one mediation she rode alone two hundred miles through the territory of a hostile neighboring tribe to wheedle the Paiutes back from the warpath. For this service she became for a few weeks a newspaper heroine. She was married fleetingly to a German named Snyder, who died, and an Army lieutenant named Bartlett, whom she left. Later still, according to an obituary notice from an old Reno newspaper, which I found pasted inside the Public Library's copy of her book, "she married a soldier named Hopkins, who accompanied her on a lecturing tour through the East and spent all the money she earned. He was a well-educated, handsome young man, and an inveterate gambler. He died some years ago." Sarah wrote "Life Among the

Piutes" on this Eastern journey. Hodge's "Handbook of American Indians," an encyclopedia and biographical dictionary issued in 1910, says that Sarah ran an Indian school at Lovelock, Nevada, which she abandoned after Hopkins' death, and died "degenerate" in Monida, Montana, in 1891, by which the biographer meant that she had gone back to living as an Indian.

In her book Sarah said that Indian wars were usually instigated by settlers who wanted to bring troops into their region so they could sell hay and cattle to the Army at inflated prices. The early Indian agents, she declared, exploited the reservations as their private domains. "Now, Dear Readers, this is the way all the Indian agents get rich," she wrote in one place, going on to cite an agent's misprisions. Another passage reads, "Mr. Mushrush, the farmer, does all his farming in the barroom at Wadsworth." (Wadsworth is a railroad town that grew up in the southern tip of the reservation.) But she did not pick on whites exclusively. Of an Indian named Captain Dave, she wrote, "He has no character whatever and could always be hired to do a wicked thing. He is my own cousin."

The Paiutes, perhaps seven thousand in all, were scattered over a territory twice as large as New York State, and never had a comprehensive tribal organization. Each band ran its own affairs. Sarah, who was both a natural press agent and an ambitious daughter, told our military that Old Winnemucca was chief of all the Paiutes, but he wasn't. He was chief of the Pyramid Lake band, which numbered about six hundred, and he had the prestige of an elder statesman among the other northern bands, but south of the Truckee he had no influence. Nevertheless, he became the most famous Paiute chief in history, and a town and a lake have been named for him: James W. Nye, who was the first governor of the Territory of Nevada, described him in 1861 as "a most intelligent and appreciative man, one who reasons well and talks like a prudent, reflective leader." De Quille stated that the name Winnemucca means "the charitable man." De Quille didn't rate the chief as highly as Nye had, however; he wrote, "He is a good-natured, kind-hearted old man, but not a man remarkable for either wisdom or cunning." A later and more scholarly observer has written that Winnemucca means "the man with a hole in his nose." These fielders' choices are the incessant lot of the amateur recorder of Paiute history.

Lake Winnemucca, the Lake of the Charitable Man with the Hole in His Nose, which is a few miles east of Pyramid, has dried up within the last twenty years, and is now what the Arabs would call a *chott*—a shimmering expanse of alkali in the arid plain. In the fat past, it was full of fish and mud hens, the latter so tame a man could go out to them on a reed raft and whack them on the head with a club. They didn't taste like mallard, but the practical Paiutes valued them more highly. "They cost nothing for cartridges," Albert Aleck, a Paiute who drives the school bus for the on-reservation pupils, told me once, during a symposium on the nutritional glories of the past. Winnemucca, a shallow lake, depended for its existence on an underground runoff from its larger neighbor. When the level of water in Pyramid Lake declined, Lake Winnemucca disappeared. So did the giant trout of Pyramid Lake, which constituted the chief gastronomic endowment of Old Winnemucca's people. The trout and a fish called the cui-ui, found nowhere else in the world (although it has relatives in certain lakes of Utah, Oregon, and India), provided a regular supply of protein that made the Pyramid Lake band the strongest, most warlike, and most carefree of all the Paiute bands. "Being thus better fed than the surrounding tribes, they were also much better developed, both physically and mentally," an early observer wrote. To their neighboring tribesmen, the Pyramid Lake Paiutes were known as "the cui-ui eaters." Other Nevada Indians, less fortunately situated, had to rely on pine nuts, berries, grass seeds, sagebrush shoots, lizards, and locusts, with a semioccasional deer or antelope. De Quille tells of talking to an old brave about sagebrush soup. "Was it good?" De Quille asked. "Yes; good all same hay for cow," the Indian said.

The surface of Pyramid Lake, which attained an altitude of 3,890 feet late in the nineteenth century, dropped progressively during a cycle of dry years, which coincided with the withdrawal of water from the Truckee for irrigation and power. A couple of years ago, the lake surface had dropped to about 3,800 feet, but since then it has gained a few hopeful feet—the result of a couple of good rainy seasons. When the lake had dropped to around 3,840 feet, the trout and cui-ui found it impossible to cross the shallows and whirlpools at the Truckee's mouth to get up the river to spawn. Government engineers installed a fish ladder, but it hasn't worked. When I was there in 1949, the cui-ui had become scarce and the trout were believed to have disappeared. "There used to be those big lake trout, with green backs and silver bellies, all pink meat," Aleck, a lean man, told me as we continued our discussion.

"And those big cutthroat trout, all rosy, with white meat, that you could only catch in the spawning season," said Martin Green, another Paiute, who was an M.P. in the 29th Division.

"And those tommy trout that used to run with the cui-ui, just pan size—you'd cut them into chunks and throw them in the skillet," said Levi Frazier, a Paiute quarter-horse trainer, who a lot of Nevadans think is also the best calf roper in the country. ("That's a little too strong," Levi himself says.)

"It was a sportmen's paradise," Aleck said. "But there were no sportmen to enjoy it. Just hungry Indians."

Fishing is favorable to contemplation; the rise among the Paiutes of the first Amerindian literary lady was no accident when viewed in the light of sumptuary determinism. Smohalla, the great prophet of the Columbia River (in the course of my supplementary readings on the Paiutes, I have met some other fascinating Indians), who enunciated the truth that man should not work, made a grudging exception in the case of fishing. "Men who work cannot dream, and wisdom comes to us in dreams," Smohalla said. But of fishing he conceded, "This work lasts only for a few weeks. . . . Besides, it is natural work and does no harm." He therefore qualified his commandment of "Thou shalt not work" with "except for a little fishing."

Every year, when the cui-ui run was over, the Paiutes would radiate from the lake in small family groups, to take advantage of the seasonal cycle of wild crops and small game. After the discovery of precious metals in Nevada, the whites entered the region in great numbers, cutting down the piñon trees for fuel and the seed-bearing grasses for fodder. The Paiutes' seasonal wanderings became potential occasions of conflict, and in order to avert them, Major Frederick Dodge, a special Indian agent, proposed in 1859 that Pyramid Lake and its shores and the delta of the Truckee be set aside as a reservation. This was not altruism, for settlers in the new territory were as vulnerable to attack as new-hatched birds; indeed, the government was extremely eager to have the Paiutes accept this solution. The Indian Commissioner, the Land Office Commissioner, and the Secretary of the Interior hastily endorsed Dodge's proposal, but even so they were not able to forestall a war that, in the estimate of an official of the Indian Bureau, "set the Territory back one year in its development." In the spring of 1860, the Pyramid Lake Indians killed three white men who had abducted and abused two Indian women. A hundred and five whites from the booming silver-rush settlement of Virginia City, fifty miles away, rode up to the lake to chastise the Indians. They were forceful fellows—whiskered vigilantes brave enough to lynch practically anybody they could catch in bed—but they found Indian-fighting a very arduous form of amusement. Winnemucca's people killed seventy-six of them, including, unfortunately, Major Ormsby. The rest arrived back at Virginia City with obsidian arrowheads embedded in their horses' rumps, and emigration began immediately. De Quille wrote,

> At Virginia City, when the news of the defeat at Pyramid Lake came, among other business transacted was the unanimous adoption of the following resolution: "Resolved, that during the next sixty days, or until the settlement of the present Indian difficulties, no claim or mining ground within the Territory shall be subject to re-location, or liable to be jumped for non-work." This gave many persons who had urgent business in California an opportunity of going over and attending to it—doubtless many started soon after voting on the resolution.

After the panic subsided, a column of United States Regulars escorted another mob of miners up to the lake, where the soldiers whipped the Indians and the miners took three scalps from corpses. The Paiutes, however, were still formidable, and on

July 19, 1861, three months after the Civil War began, Governor Nye wrote to Washington:

> I deem it of the utmost importance that friendly relations should be maintained with all the tribes along the line of the telegraph, overland mail, and pony express, as they are now the only modes of communication with the States and the home government. I assume that the government so regards it, and shall exert myself to the utmost to secure so desirable and necessary an object. . . . The [Paiutes], as well as the Shoshones, are warlike tribes, and able, from the peculiar section and region they occupy, to make great trouble if once excited to arms. . . . If so, it will require a soldier to every telegraph post, and a company of soldiers at each stage station through the entire Indian country to preserve peace.
>
> In order to secure permanent peace with these several tribes, I am quite satisfied that some definite line of policy must be pursued. Several have been suggested, but the one most advantageous to the government and to the Indians, as it appears to me, is this: They are by nature herdsmen, and well adapted to that pursuit, and learn with great facility to perform all the necessary care to the successful breeding of cattle, which must form the great staple of their living and support. I would recommend that the government furnish for them a quantity of cows, and the agent can instruct them in a short time so as to enable them to raise all the beef they will require. Most of the Pah-Utes are good mowers, and are acquainted with the curing of the wild grass that grows on the reservation, and sufficient grows to keep their cattle through the winter, if properly secured. I would also recommend that the government furnish them with some brood mares, so that they can grow their own horses of a better quality than the miserable ones they now have.

Nye's subordinate, an agent named Wasson, called the Paiutes "of all the Indians I am acquainted with, the most susceptible of acquiring the arts of civilized life."

It affords me great pleasure [Wasson wrote to Nye in 1861] to inform you that the Pah-Utes, since the unfortunate difficulties with them more than a year ago, have behaved themselves with the utmost propriety till about the middle of April last, submitting to the grossest outrages upon them committed by villainous whites, [and] having their men shot and their horses stolen on several occasions without offering to resent the outrages themselves. About that time, they assembled in council at the reservation of Walker River to the number of about three thousand. A portion of the most warlike from the interior, numbering perhaps two or three hundred, influenced by white enemies to the peace and harmony of the country, were disposed to create disturbances, drove off the interpreter, and otherwise behaved very badly. I succeeded, however, in quieting them, and they are now dispersed over the country, engaged in their usual occupations, hunting and gathering seeds, etc., for winter use. . . .

It is almost absolutely necessary, in order to preserve their good will, that some more presents from the government be issued to them before long, and I would suggest that a few ornaments to please their fancy be selected with other articles of more utility; and the superintendent should be provided with ample means to assist them in case of severe winter, an occurrence by no means unusual here, of which we can have no previous warning. . . . This policy will insure peace at an expense of not more than five dollars per Indian for the first year and three dollars for the subsequent year. There is not a Pah-Ute warrior in the tribe who is not capable of costing the government five thousand dollars a year in the event of war, to say nothing of the consequent loss of life and the retarding of the development of the country, obstructing of the mail and telegraph lines, and the cutting off of emigration entirely.

If we assume that there were three hundred warriors in the Pyramid Lake band in Wasson's time, they could have caused a million and a half dollars' worth of damage annually. And if we assume that it would have taken five thousand soldiers five years to track them down—a modest estimate, considering the ratio of soldiers to Indians employed in the Apache and Bannock wars—we may fix the total expense arbitrarily, but not unreasonably, at twenty-five million dollars, plus interest at five per cent from 1865 to 1955. From all this, we may justly conclude that the establishment of the Pyramid Lake Reservation was one of the greatest bargains in administrative history—especially since the Indians owned the land before we got there.

The *quid-pro-quo* policy succeeded in placating the Indians, but almost immediately white Nevadans began to chisel the *quid*. One wrong that Mrs. Hopkins complained of was the encroachment of white men upon the reservation, which began as soon as the land around the lake had been ordered surveyed for a reservation, in 1859. Nye, visiting Winnemucca in 1861, discovered some squatters already there and wrote to the Secretary of the Interior, in Washington: "On the [southern] end of this reservation I found two ranchers and five white settlers. I here instructed the agent to warn them off, which he has done. I understand they have promised to go as soon as they can secure the crops growing on their several ranches." Ninety-four years later, their successors in interest are still there.

An old man named T. G. Herman, one of the earliest settlers on the reservation, told an Indian Service inspector named O'Fallon in 1909 that he himself had been warned off by Wasson in 1861. This, said O'Fallon, "established the vital fact that the original white inhabitants of the disputed land were fully cognizant of the fact that they had taken Indian land." Herman's admittedly illegal claim formed part of the squatter lands until they were repossessed, some eighty years later. Another tract in dispute, known as the Hill Ranch, was the subject of a report by an Army lieutenant named Lee, who served as a special Indian agent in 1869. "The land was settled by an industrious Indian named Truckee John," Lee wrote. "He improved the land by fencing and building a house, raising horses, grass, grain, and some vegetables. His prosperity aroused the jealousy and hatred of a mean, worthless, and villainous white man named Fleming, who brutally murdered the Indian near his ranch on July 4, 1867. Afterwards, Indians were afraid to locate on it lest they meet the same fate, no cognizance having been taken of the dastardly murder by the civil or other authorities."

During my stay at the lake in 1949, I met several Winnemuccas, even though I never happened to hear of the literary Sarah. One of the current crop is Harry, a stocky man who drives the school bus between Nixon, which is the reservation village, and Fernley, which has the nearest junior high school. (The reservation school, which Aleck drives for, goes through only the sixth grade.) Harry is a hard man to figure at the stick game, which is something like our match game and was the Paiutes' favorite form of gambling until some soldier slipped them a pack of playing cards and they invented Paiute poker. De Quille wrote, long ago, "Old Winnemucca was an inveterate gambler. . . . [He was] known to lose all his ponies, all his blankets and arms, and, in fact, everything he possessed, down to a breech-clout, at a single sitting." In the stick game, you try to tell which fists two other fellows are holding four antelope bones in. There are two plain-white bones and two striped ones. Whenever you guess a bone wrong, the holding side scores a point. When you guess right, your team gets possession of the bones and a chance to score. Ten sticks are used as counters, and when one side has them all, it picks up the stakes of silver dollars. To disturb the guesser's concentration, the men holding the bones sing. Harry Winnemucca is the most disturbing singer in the Great Basin. This Winnemucca has a round, jolly face, like a Calabrian extortionist's. A kinsman of his named Avery Winnemucca is a more serious sort, who has inherited with his name a strong awareness of wrongs and claims. Avery, who looks like a straight-featured Japanese, has a white-collar job off the reservation, but he comes home weekends, and he is the most oratorical spokesman for the Pyramid Lake Paiutes, who are now an incorporated tribe.

When I first heard talk about the Pyramid Lake dispute, I took it for granted that the demonstrable fact that the Paiutes had been living on the land for more than thirty-five hundred years would have considerable bearing on their right to it. But on reading printed records of hearings that have been held before Congressional committees investigating the matter, I learned that this tenancy gave them no legal claim, since the Spaniards, who were the first white men to declare sovereignty over western North America, had recognized no such rights. Nor had the Mexicans, who succeeded the Spaniards, nor had the government of the United States when it took over from Mexico, in 1848. United States District Court Judge Edward Farrington, ruling on the ownership of this very reservation in 1918, said, "While the Indians have always claimed they were the original owners of the soil, the validity of their claim has never been conceded. In the Treaty of Guadalupe-Hidalgo, such property rights as they had were recognized and safeguarded, but it does not appear in the pleadings that the Paiutes prior to that treaty or prior to the execution of the executive order establishing the reservation had acquired any title, possession, or right of possession in or to the land in controversy." In my previous legal reading, admittedly skimpy, I had never encountered this theory, the Preëminent Right of the First Trespasser. But it is consistent with much Indian Law, a legal euphemism for the statutes imposed on Indians by whites while the whites were skinning the Indians. Farrington's decision was always cited with approbation by the late United States Senator Patrick A. McCarran, the perennial proponent of the squatters' claims.

As recently as 1924, there were twelve squatters occupying land on the reservation. In that year, Congress passed a bill permitting them to buy the lands they had long enjoyed without payment. Seven paid up, and five made a first payment and then defaulted. The Indians were not consulted about the sale. By 1936, there had been a considerable change in thinking about Indians. For one thing, they had been voting for a dozen years and had begun to get the hang of it; for another, Franklin D. Roosevelt was in, with Harold L. Ickes as Secretary of the Interior and John Collier, who for years had been executive secretary of the American Indian Defense Association, as Indian Commissioner. Ickes called time on the five recalcitrant squatters, and they almost immediately began to profess their eagerness to pay up, now that it was too late. Land values, of course, were rising. Of the five claimants, three, all named Ceresola, were brothers, and another, a man named De Paoli, was their half brother. The fifth was the Garaventa Land & Livestock Co., owned by several Garaventas incorporated under that name. All the squatters were Nevada-born and of Genoese origin. Some of the land they were on was indisputably theirs— their predecessors in interest had bought it in fee simple, or outright, from the infant State of Nevada back in the eighteen-sixties. But more of it was reservation land they had more or less casually spread out on over the years. Banks in Reno held mortgages on the squatters' lands, including those rightfully belonging to the Indians. In 1937, the banks, the squatters, and the squatters' relatives all joined in sicking McCarran, then in his first term, on the Indians.

In urging the adoption of his first bill, which provided that the land should be given to the squatters, the Senator pointed out that the mortgage owners "would like fair play in this matter, because they have money involved," and then went on, "But that is really out of the question. This question involves the homes and hearth-fires of these five poor, unfortunate families." When that bill failed, he introduced successors, in 1939, 1941, 1943, 1945, 1947, 1949, 1951, and 1953. On returning home from Pyramid Lake in 1949, I took to reading printed records of the hearings on McCarran's various bills, much as one reads a serialized story. Not only were they good reading but each succeeding bill on this obscure matter seemed more extraordinary psychologically, for McCarran was gradually being projected by seniority into the Senatorial foreground. There he functioned as a spokesman for Pan American Airways (the chosen-instrument policy), for the distilling industry in wartime (it wanted more alcohol for use in the manufacture of liquor), for General Franco (McCarran eventually got him almost a quarter of a billion dollars), and for the world silver interests. Compared to these combobulations, his small Nevada deal might have been expected to seem to him a waste of time. Nevertheless, he persisted, doubtless in the spirit of Major General George Custer, a forerunner of his in Indian-baiting. As Major General Terry de la Mesa Allen, an old cavalryman, once told me, "Custer got killed. But on account of what happened to him, the United States Cavalry got the repeating rifle. With the rifle, they cleaned up the Sioux. And now Custer sits up in Heaven thumbing his nose at those damn Indians." I concluded that the Senator, a holder of the Grand Cross of the Order of Isabella the Catholic (Spain), did not want to go to Heaven with any Paiutes here below thumbing their noses at him. It tickled me that opponents so unpretentious as the Paiutes could hold the old fulminator at bay when he had succeeded in imposing on the whole country his set of entrance requirements for visitors to the United States.

Just about a year ago, I decided I would go back to the lake to see how the quiet battle was progressing. I was also possessed by a strong desire to see the lake itself again and to renew acquaintance with a fellow out there named Harry Drackert, who has taken to raising race horses. As reading matter for the trip, I took with me a record of the hearings before the Senate Committee on Interior and Insular Affairs on s.17, which was the title of McCarran's Pyramid Lake Bill of 1949. The Senator's zeal had outlived both the Senate and the House Committees on Indian Affairs, which had been abolished in 1947 and their function turned over to Interior and Insular. I also noted other important changes in the cast since the 1943 hearings, the last I had been privileged to read about in full. Commissioner Collier, who played Dauntless Durham to McCarran's Desperate Desmond in the earlier productions, had retired in 1945. He had served twelve years as Commissioner of Indian Affairs—the longest tenure on record, but not long enough to discourage McCarran. Nevada's Senator James G. Scrugham, McCarran's junior and his relentless opponent in 1943, had died, and Nevada's Congressman Maurice J. Sullivan, who fought the 1943 bill in the House, was no longer a member of Congress. Mr. Ickes, after a run of thirteen years, had been succeeded as Secretary of the Interior by Julius Krug.

The United States, which had entered the Second World War under the shadow of s.13, the Senator's 1941 bill to take the land from the Indians, had emerged triumphant from that struggle only to find s.22, the Senator's 1945 bill, still pending. In 1944, after the Circuit Court of Appeals ruled that the Indians owned the land, the Supreme Court had refused to hear any more about the matter. McCarran's s.30 (1947) had perished in the first solidly Republican Congress since Hoover's of 1928; this was evidence of a bipartisan point of view on at least one item of legislation. All these disappointments and mutations, which might have discouraged a man less indefatigably combative than the Senator, had but whetted his appetite for the annihilation of his opponents.

The script of the 1949 revival showed that the Senator had found a helper, in the person of his new junior colleague— United States Senator George (Molly) Malone, a Republican. McCarran, though a Democrat, had never been able to agree with any Democratic colleague. Malone's election had come in the administration ebb year of 1946. It was an election that McCarran did nothing to prevent, and Malone was humbly grateful. The script began with the familiar text of the bill, the gist of which was to allow the Ceresolas, De Paolis, and Garaventas to complete the payments they had defaulted on around 1929—a matter of twenty-two thousand dollars, all told, plus interest—in return for which they would receive patents to the land. In the center of the stage as the curtain rose was Senator Ernest McFarland, of Arizona, presiding in the place of Senator Joseph C. O'Mahoney, of Wyoming, the chairman, who was absent. Senator McFarland read a long letter from Secretary Krug, reviewing the Congressional and judicial history of the case, right through the Supreme Court's wave of the hand denoting "out." Krug opposed the bill. After the Supreme Court's dismissal of the case, the Paiutes had repossessed the land in controversy, but the settlers, whose legally owned adjoining property gave them control over the irrigation ditches, had shut off the Indians' water supply. It was Krug's idea that Congress ought to acquire the land the settlers still held—at a mutually agreeable price, if possible, and by condemnation, if not—and give it to the Indians, thus ending the dispute over water rights. Next to appear on stage was William Zimmerman, Jr., Assistant Commissioner of Indian Affairs. While Zimmerman, lacking Collier's prestige and rank, was polite to the McCarran forces, he had to point out that the Interior Department, acting for and with the Indians, had won all along, right from the time the Senator introduced his original bill, s.840, in the early months of Roosevelt's second administration, when James J. Braddock was still heavyweight champion of the world. Zimmerman held the stage alone for but a moment. Then Senator Malone entered, like a clown walk-around heralding the entrance of a death-defying aerialist. "Mr. Zimmerman, I am sorry I missed the beginning of your testimony," Malone said. "If you have not already done so, I would like you to go far enough back to give the Committee an idea of what this situation is about."

Zimmerman, thinking, no doubt, of the mountains of volumes of research that had been reduced to their essentials in two hundred and fifty closely printed pages of the reports on the 1937 and 1943 hearings, tried desperately to avoid going into all that. Senator McFarland and his fellow committee members, plainly sharing his alarm, assured Malone that it was all in the record. Malone, however, was implacable. McFarland suggested that Malone tell the story and let Zimmerman ask *him* questions. Malone ducked. He said that, being an engineer, he knew the terrain but not "the facts."

Senator Robert Kerr, of Oklahoma, then read a letter from N. B. Johnson, a justice of the Supreme Court of Oklahoma and the president of the National Congress of American Indians. (There is a whale of a big Indian vote in Oklahoma.) Johnson wrote that his organization hoped the bill would be killed in committee. "We believe that all peoples of these United States who have submitted their disputes to the highest court of the land should be secure in the feeling that the rights so determined will be protected," he declared. "The Indians are entitled to the same protection of the Fifth Amendment as non-Indians. The government cannot take private property for private use. There is no equity in the squatters' position. . . . The picture they like to paint of having roots in the land that are deeper than the Indians' is pure, window-dressing."

Senator Malone said he wondered if Judge Johnson had ever been to Pyramid Lake. "Harm is done by good people, well-intentioned people, who are thousands of miles away from the place," he added. (On-the-spot research is a Malone forte; he keeps a map of the world on one wall of his office in the Senate Office Building, so he can point out the places he has been. "Do you know the difference between a Moslem and a Mussulman?" he once asked me, pointing to Cairo on the map. I confessed I didn't—they are synonyms, of course—and he said, "A Moslem will eat meat, but a Mussulman won't. That's the kind of thing you wouldn't learn sitting in an office." It happens not to be true, too; the good Senator must have had in the back of his noodle something he had once heard about the vegetarianism of Hindus.)

McFarland then read into the record a considerable portion of what McCarran had said about the lands at the 1937 hearings, and Kerr, perhaps thinking of that Indian vote back home, read into the record in rebuttal the 1942 opinion of the Circuit Court of Appeals ruling that the land belonged to the Paiutes.

At that moment, the star entered.

SENATOR KERR [perceiving McCarran]: Come in, Senator, and sit right here.

SENATOR MCCARRAN: If I do not make a statement now, I do not know when I am going to be able to do so, and yet I can hardly now because they are calling for me. . . . I would like to put the map up here.

SENATOR KERR [in a last, futile effort to postpone the inevitable]: May I call your attention to the fact that your statement is there in the record?

SENATOR MCCARRAN: I want to go into a little more detail before the Committee. The river meanders and flows in here, and these lands have been occupied by the Indians for a long time. The Paiute tribe, as reported by the Indian Agency, in the early history of the tribe was not an agrarian tribe; it is a fishing and hunting tribe. . . . The first white settlers to come into this picture at all, gentlemen, were soldiers who had crossed the plains with General Winfield Scott Hancock. [One of those soldiers was the Senator's own father, also named Pat McCarran, who was an immigrant from Ireland.]

When those soldiers' enlistments were over, some of them
came on to this river and took up pieces of land. . . .
    Please understand that in those days there was no Indian
reservation. It was not until 1874, by the edict of President
Grant, that the Indian reservation was established [This
theory had been demolished by the court seven years
before.] . . . but where it was established, to this day I am
unable to determine.

Here McCarran complained that the original map of the reservation had been lost. He thought there was every likelihood that it
bore little resemblance to the map that accompanied President
Grant's confirmation of the reservation boundaries. "I am con-
fident that if that [original] survey ever shows up, it will show an
entirely different reservation," he said.

    Members of the Committee [McCarran continued], the white
    settlers who are in there now are all Italian farmers. . . . These
    people lived, married and gave in marriage, nurtured their
    first-born and buried their dead. [This echoed portions of his
    1937 and 1943 speeches, but I felt I could read it many times
    more with pleasure, it was so beautiful.] Members of the
    Committee, no Indian ever set a foot on those lands to take
    sagebrush off the land or to put a drop of water on them. . . .
    These lands were levelled, cleared of sagebrush and put
    into . . . standing crops of alfalfa and grain. It is now stated
    that the Indians shall come in here and live alongside of them
    when, as a matter of fact, it is utterly impossible, because the
    water that goes on any one of these lands comes through
    ditches that were constructed and were the private property
    of these settlers. And the water that will irrigate those lands
    was water adjudicated to them by the Federal Court of the
    United States.

At this juncture, Senator Malone, whom I imagined standing
by like the stooge who used to hold a cake of ice in his arms for

Van Hoven, the Mad Magician, intervened to feed his patron a line:

> SENATOR MALONE: Mr. Chairman, I have a question on that point. Senator McCarran, if these lands were adjudged and found to belong to the Indians, who, under our state law, would own the water and could transfer it? . . .
> SENATOR McCARRAN [with the speed of well-trained lightning]: The white settlers to whom the decree allocates the water could dispose of the water that would go on these lands. And to be very frank with you, some of the farmers up the river there have been talking with these white settlers as to whether or not, if they lost on this thing, they will sell their water to them. All they have to do is sell the water to me or John Smith or Bill Jones up the river, and the water master [a federal official who allocates irrigation water] will take it away from these ditches here and divert it upstream.
> SENATOR MALONE: Then, Senator McCarran, if that were done, and I agree with you that it could be done under the state law of Nevada, and all other states that have that theory of law, with which I am familiar, what value would attach to those lands without the water?
> SENATOR McCARRAN: These lands without the water are utterly useless; they are utterly useless.

McFarland then asked McCarran's opinion of Secretary Krug's alternative proposition—that the government acquire the lands of the settlers by purchase or condemnation. I could have warned him not to do it; McCarran was a highly combustible senator. "Now, my understanding of that condemnation is that it cannot be resorted to under the Constitution of this country for private use," said McCarran. "That is what they want to do, is to condemn those people and throw them out into the cold world, where they and their families have lived and paid taxes for years, and where no Indian ever set foot upon that land, either in private or public ownership; no Indian put a plow in that land, Mr. Chairman. . . ."

"I wanted to say that the Senator served as a Supreme Court justice of our state," Senator Malone eventually interposed, "and he is entirely familiar with the law, and when he makes a statement with respect to the law, it is not to be taken lightly."

Kerr inquired if there hadn't been a court decision to the effect that the Indians owned the land, and McCarran replied, "I say no."

Kerr then read the Circuit Court decision again, but McCarran brushed it aside.

> I have read that before [he said]. I am familiar with that, but that does not meet the situation at all. . . . I am sawing right through everything and saying that Congress has the perfect right to grant these people the right to pay up on the original contract. . . . Now I am ready to answer any questions that are propounded. I have stated the case, as I see it, as I have seen it all my life, because I was reared within twenty-five miles of this locality here. . . . It seems to me that the situation presents something that the Congress must do; if this were in some other locality, gentlemen, you would have bloodshed over there with respect to this thing, which I never want to see happen. Someday or another, fire is going to blaze and break loose down there. Some hothead is going to lose his head, and then what? Today [the Indians] are fencing Ceresola around, they are fencing out his house, in which his family lives; they are fencing out his stockyards, in which he feeds his cattle.

Reviewing McCarran's performance, I felt that while it had gained in bite, and perhaps in bark, it lacked the ingenuous bonhomie of his 1937 interpretation and the suave majesty of his 1943 reading. As for Malone, while he evinced undeniable comic talent, I thought he and McCarran should decide which of the two was the straight man. I pictured McCarran still rolling up his map and milking the audience for curtain calls when a new member of the cast appeared—James E. Curry, attorney for the Indians of the Pyramid Lake Reservation and for the National Congress of American Indians. He said that the Paiutes had "original title," and, moreover, had been described by an agent in 1859 as undoubtedly the most interesting and docile Indians on the continent. "I say that," Mr. Curry went on, "because I do not wish Mr. Winnemucca to be embarrassed in testifying, or for it to be believed that his people also do not have some equities on their side." With that, he produced as a witness my acquaintance Avery Winnemucca.

Before Avery got under way, however, Senator Malone made a highly magnanimous speech. "Mr. Chairman," he said, "before we proceed with Mr. Winnemucca, I want to say that . . . I have known these Indians, who have come from my own state, for a considerable time, and I want to say further, Mr. Curry, that I myself . . . [intend] to introduce a bill that will make Indians people. . . . As a matter of fact, they are just as intelligent as we are. . . . So when you come here as a character witness for the Indians, it is lost on me."

"Thank you, Senator," said Curry.

Avery took a longer forensic windup than Albert Aleck, his brother-in-law, who played the Indian part in the 1943 production. Avery began by telling the committee about the battle of Pyramid Lake, giving his great-grandfather, Chief Winnemucca, none the worst of the score. Chief Winnemucca, Avery said, had told his tribe that "they cannot fight the white men, and might just as well make some kind of an arrangement to be courteous with them." But messengers reached the chief with reports that relatives of the kidnapped Indian women had killed several whites and burned their station. So the chief said, "Well, then, you have to use your own discretion on this matter, as my talk to you has failed." After that, Avery said, the Indians regretfully annihilated Major Ormsby and the other white men. He added that—"contradicting Senator Pat McCarran"—Indians had at one time definitely farmed along the Truckee River.

There at . . . what is known as the Hill Ranch [Avery said], in 1867, July 4—this date stands out vividly among the Indians —an Indian by the name of Truckee John farmed in that section. He actually farmed. Water was conveyed in through

83

ditches, and that is before any white man was there. There was no white man there. The whole town of Wadsworth was a battlefield . . . and on this July 4, some white men who wanted that field, because it was all irrigated, they killed Truckee John, shot him in the back, killed him outright because they wanted his field.

And at that same time we had a beautiful lake which is called Pyramid Lake, widely known all over the world for its wonderful fishing and fish. Pat McCarran has used this, and said that we were fishermen, and we were not agriculturists. . . . His statement is not really strictly in accordance with the facts. As I have said, my ancestors had really farmed in the various sections of this Truckee River. . . . Now that our fishing has been ruined by the agriculturists who have drained our lake for irrigation, we have no more fish. Of course, then, we, too, have turned now to a modern way of living, due to the fact that we could not make a living on fishing, so now we have turned to cattle raising. We have also turned into agriculturists. . . . If the court had told us that these settlers or squatters were rightly on this land, we would have gladly accepted the court's decision, but the court found in this case that the land was ours, and we had the right to that land, and have the right to use that. But the white man somehow or other, or maybe it is the politicians, they do not seem to have accepted this right of the court's decision. Instead they ask you to deprive us of our rights which the court says was ours. This puts us in a kind of puzzling situation.

Senator McFarland asked Avery if the Paiutes were farming the repossessed land. "The repossessed land, as Senator McCarran has said, we did fence that in, but we coöperated with them," Avery replied. "We did not completely fence them all in. We have left opening gaps such as to his barn. . . . We would not do anything to hurt them."

My study of Senator McCarran's maneuvers sustained me during most of my train ride across the country. On the morning of my arrival in Reno, I checked in at the Riverside Hotel. From my room, I tried to call the Senator, who used to live at the Riverside when he was home among the grass roots, but I was told that he was away on a shooting trip in Oregon with Senator Cordon, a Republican. So I telephoned Drackert, who runs a guest ranch on Pyramid Lake, and asked him to come in and get me at the Riverside bar. A soft October rain was falling, and Reno, with its nine-thousand-foot mountain towering over it, reminded me of a Swiss valley town; in summer, the sun is so bright that the scene makes me think of the Atlas Mountains. Adjoining the bar is the hotel casino, a more dangerous place to browse in than a bookshop. I ventured a couple of stacks of quarter chips on a wheel and found that nothing had changed; there were still no zeros. I asked the pretty girl dealer if any had showed up since 1949, and hurt tears glistened in her doelike eyes. "I turned it up three times in a row three times yesterday afternoon," she said. "Why did you stay away so long?" ("We teach our girls always to root for the customer," Mort Wertheimer, one of the brothers who run the casino, once told me. "The customers like it, and the situation is unchanged.")

I went back to the bar, and when Harry arrived, I could see he was in fine fettle. He walked in at a lope, with his back straight, as if he were riding his legs. His face had a carefree glow. It was the off season, he reminded me, and there was only one postulant for a divorce out at the ranch. This left him free to concentrate on horses, which interest him more. The women waiting out divorces are his cash crop in summertime, but it is not on record that any woman has ever won even an allowance race at Santa Anita, and they have no form you can depend upon. Harry said that he had six yearlings at the Washoe County Fair Grounds track, which was just outside town on the way to the lake. A fellow named Al Hetrick was legging them up for the late-winter races in California, galloping them easily on the dirt track, which had been torn up by stock-car races and motorcycle daredevils.

On our way to the ranch, we stopped at the track to pick up a trailer and load it with a yearling that a veterinary had told Harry was too big and sprawly to be worked yet. Harry had me look at every one of his yearlings, all of them by a stallion he had at the ranch named Andy K. They were out of a Kiev mare, a Wise Counselor mare, and some mares I have forgotten. He vaulted onto their bare backs to show me how well he had broken them. The lessons had not included trailer manners, though, and the overgrown yearling—a brown—fought to keep his four feet on the ground. Harry got in first and pulled, while two stable guineas drew a rope across the yearling's hams and imparted a forward motion to him. "Come on, damn you," Harry said. "You got to learn sometime."

When we had the yearling loaded, we started out across the Nevada hills, which in the early twilight were the color of dark plums. As the car's lights illuminated the surface of the road, with its tessellation of flattened jack rabbits, I asked Harry how the row over the water rights was coming along, and he said that nothing had happened. "The Indians are all busy getting ready for Admission Day down to Carson," he said. "There's supposed to be a big Indian parade the second day of the ceremonies." Admission Day is the anniversary of the day Nevada joined the Union—October 31, 1864. "The Admission Day committee hired a fellow from Hollywood to write a pageant, and there is a Hungarian girl from there come up to teach the Indians dances," Harry went on. "They're holding a rehearsal in the gymnasium over at Nixon tonight. All Indians in the parade in costume will get fifteen dollars, with five dollars extra for a papoose and the same if mounted on a horse. Avery Winnemucca is the assistant director of the pageant, and Martin Green is marshal of the parade." I asked Harry if Martin was still the reservation policeman, as he had been when I was there before. Harry said no, and explained that Martin's experience as an M.P. during the war had kind of disqualified him for home service. Every time a man and his wife started a little family squall, Martin would bounce them both into the brig, as if they were German prisoners. This had detracted from the popularity of all Martin's relatives on the reservation. Also, Martin had taken to reading the regulations, and he would impound the cattle of white ranchers if he found them on the reservation eating Indian grass. Naturally, no justice of the peace would support any such nonsense as that, and so Martin had quit. "He couldn't get back to a civilian point of view," Harry said. We reached the ranch at the hour of the apéritif. Even though it was the off season, the bar had some trade. Harry's wife, Joan, was behind the counter, wearing a white buckskin rodeo-parade outfit that had been trimmed with light blue beadwork by Nellie Calico, one of the reservation matriarchs. Peggy Marsh, the barmaid, who had gone out to Nevada in 1929 to write a novel, was sitting at a card table composing a letter to the Jockey Club on Harry's behalf about the lip tattoo on a horse named Piute Chief. (Harry sticks to the De Quille spelling.) Pancho, a sad Mexican section hand who works on the railroad back of the ranch, was in his usual corner, trying to buy everybody beer. Pancho has never learned that the way to keep people drinking with you is to let all hands buy a round; he feels this is incompatible with his grandeur. Now and then, some oaf appears in the bar who is willing to exploit Pancho's suicidal munificence, but Joan and Harry devise some protective dodge, like telling the man they cannot serve him because he is drunk. Jimmy, a temporarily stove-up rodeo bull-rider from Las Cruces, New Mexico, was playing a tune called "Big Mamou" on the juke box. But most of the noise was being contributed by Pedro, the Filipino cook, who was working the dime and nickel slot machines concurrently, one with each hand—stuffing them with coins and then banging the levers down so fast it sounded like an old railroad train lumbering over a rough stretch of track. Pedro is about four feet six, under a white toque a foot and a half high. When he comes down on the levers, he lifts himself off the floor, chattering in Filipino Castilian mixed with a tongue I took to be Tagalog until the first time I talked to him; it turned out to be his personal form of English. Now and then, there was a third noise—five, ten, fourteen, or eighteen coins cascading down into the metal underlip of one of the machines—but this afforded no intermission. Pedro is a jackpot man, and doesn't stop to scoop up his lesser windfalls until he has used up all his original capital. Then he chucks the winnings in. When he is clean, he hops up on the bar rail and takes an advance on his pay. Joan has given up trying to dissuade him from this. If

87

she does try, he accuses the house of wanting to freeze him out just before he hits the pot. He threatens to quit. This poses a tough problem, because, on the one hand, Pedro is the best cook Joan has ever had, and, on the other, Joan figures that if he keeps on losing, he may kill himself. She is mighty happy when she hears a jackpot drop; usually it is the nickel machine—seven-fifty. Pedro is all smiles then, even though it has cost him twenty. He offers to buy drinks for the house. After that, his frenzy appeased, he goes off to the kitchen to rescue the victuals from Viola, the maid. On this particular night, the jackpot fell while I was still on my second Scotch, and Joan's facial muscles relaxed. "Now I know we'll get something to eat," she said.

"Easy when you know how, don't it?" Pedro asked, coming up to the bar with his apron full of nickels.

"I'll take that seven-fifty off your tab," Joan said. He went away happy.

The noise hadn't affected the other people in the bar, most of whom were Indians I remembered from 1949. They were drinking what they pleased, and this was a change for the better. Congress at its most recent session had passed a law that freed Indians from the ghastly discrimination of being denied alcohol. The Indians at the bar were Albert Aleck, Warren Tobey, Martin Green, and Avery Winnemucca, all members of the Pyramid Lake Tribal Council, and with them was the lady dance instructor from Hollywood, who had an Italian-boy haircut and powerful calves. Aleck has a thin, ascetic face and wears glasses. Tobey is a slender, graceful man with heavy-lidded eyes. Green is wide-shouldered and powerful, with the face of a good-natured Aztec idol. Avery Winnemucca, as I have said, looks a trifle Japanese. All the faces were different, but they also possessed a common difference from other faces—and that includes other kinds of Indians' faces.

I shook hands all around. The Indians introduced me to the lady from Hollywood (who whispered ecstatically, "They are such preemie-teeves! Real peasants!") and to the sole *pensionnaire*, who was there for the usual Reno reasons. She was a blonde named Anna Lou. She smiled and said, "*Ahm* not at oal intellectual," after which she turned from me to drench the choreographer in a gaze as sweet and cold as an ice-cream soda with two dabs of whipped cream. "Ah don't see how you'll be able to *stand* little ole me!"

A shadow crossed the Hollywood woman's face, and she hitched up her pants, which, with a man's sweater and ballet slippers, composed her *costume de soirée*. "I am sure you are *vairy* intelligent when you weesh to be," she told Anna Lou.

The Paiutes gazed with neutral interest, as if watching a fight between a magpie and a bull snake.

Anna Lou said sweetly, "Tha only talent Ah hayv is just fo being takun cayuh of." She snuggled a lavender fur cape about her bare shoulders and shook her head in gentle self-deprecation, which imparted a wistful swing to her long earrings.

Sticking to the theme of my journey, I asked Avery Winnemucca how the dispute over the water rights was coming along. "I guess we're stuck until old Pat conks out," he answered.

"Old people used to talk about those lands when I was a boy," Aleck said. He is a serious, New Englandish kind of Indian—a local-history buff. "Used to talk about what we'd do with them when we got them. Those people all in happy hunting grounds." He grinned. Paiutes consider such literary Indianisms corny, and use them only for laughs. "When we go to Washington, we see plenty of buck. Buck they pass. But back when my father had a little farm down by Wadsworth and a white man wanted it, they got him off fast enough. The agent came down to the house one night and said, 'Here's twenty dollars. Get out.' My old man got out."

"Didn't he put up any argument?" I asked.

"No," Aleck said. "Those old Indians didn't know any better."

The immediate business in hand, however, was the production of the pageant, which had been written by an Englishman from Hollywood and was strictly noncontroversial. The activities in the gymnasium at Nixon that evening, the Hollywood girl told me, would be a combination of tryout and rehearsal.

The Paiutes, as I knew from my researches in the Library, have never been spectacular dancers; their standard tribal dance was a counterclockwise walk in a circle, men and women alternated and holding hands. During the Ghost Dance religious excitement of 1890, they sometimes kept this up for five days and nights, singing a lyric that went, as I recall from my reading, "The snow lies there; the Milky Way lies there." The Ghost Dance religion began among the Paiutes. Its prophet, Wovoka, was one of them—from the Walker River Reservation, near Carson City. The Ghost Dance he enjoined on his disciples was just this old Paiute form of ring-around-a-rosy—a walkaround that, however rich in spiritual values, was no Agnes de Mille number. I anticipated that the choreographer would have trouble pepping it up.

When I arrived at the Nixon gymnasium, the dance director was coping with this difficulty. "One, two, *sree,* four; one, two, *sree,* four!" she shouted as she stamped about the basketball floor, leading a line of giggling younger Paiute matrons in beautifully tailored and quite unhistoric buckskin costumes. The matrons wore on their backs conical baskets full of berries or piñon nuts, and I supposed that this was some sort of traditional Mary Wigman harvest dance. The gymnasium, a vast cheesebox of a building, was unheated, because the Indian Service had removed the furnace and installed it in a building on another reservation, fifty miles away. Only the stamping choreographer seemed to be warm. The high-school set, in windbreakers and jeans, sat around the edges of the hall, whistling at the dancers. Nothing amuses a Paiute more than the sight of another Paiute dressed as an Indian.

When the choreographer had finished with the women, whom she left prostrated with laughter, she summoned the men for the war dance. The war dancers, most of whom were slightly purple by this time, sprang into action with what seemed to me satisfactory dynamism; they were crazy to get warm. They hollered and shuffled, yelled like the wild Indians they had seen in the movies, shadowboxed, and did calisthenics, but the Hollywood girl was not satisfied. The only one who pleased her was a fellow who had been in the Seabees in the South Pacific, where he had picked up a couple of Papuan steps. As for the rest, she cried, there was no *pattern* in their dance, and she called for silence. Then, holding her septum between thumb and forefinger, she bent her head in meditation. The pattern came to her. As it shaped up, it was a kind of jumping square dance. "They haven't *had* a war dance since 1860," I said to her, in palliation of the Paiutes' deficiency. "Ah," she said. "Zat explains it. Zay have forgotten."

The next morning, Martin Green called for me in his station wagon and drove me over to the disputed lands. Leaving Harry's place, we skirted the western shore of the lake on the way to Nixon. The road was familiar to me by daylight. It plays an involved tag with a branch line of the Southern Pacific, which continues south toward Wadsworth, while the road goes east into the Indian town at the foot of the lake. There was to be a cattle auction at Nixon that day; the corrals were full of Indian Herefords, and the lunch counter in Abe & Sue's store, where we stopped for a cup of coffee, already had a non-Indian clientele of stockmen and dealers. Abe, who is the most businesslike Paiute on the reservation, looked happy. When his customers sell their cattle, they pay at least a chunk on their tabs. Prices were at their lowest in many years. "Ten-cent beef" was the grim forecast. (Actually, steers went at thirteen cents; only old cows went at under a dime. As the auctioneer says, it's everybody's guess and everybody's gamble.)

After we had finished our coffee, Martin and I got back in the station wagon and headed for Wadsworth, about fifteen miles to the south. The reservation is shaped like an elongated frying pan, and Wadsworth is in the tip of the handle. Two miles below Nixon, the road rejoined the railroad, and then the two more or less paralleled each other. To the east, the land rose abruptly from the Truckee, forming what Westerners call a bench. We were in the frying-pan handle now, where the reservation is only four miles across. "That's the land McCarran is always claiming we could irrigate, and let the settlers keep our good land," Martin said. "He tells us we have a water right for all these acres. But in the summer there isn't enough water in the river for the ditches we have working now. And here there are no ditches." The benchland was dotted with Indian cattle and horses; the cattle were fair Herefords, the horses a coarse lot—not much better than the "miserable ones" of Governor Nye's time. There are wild horses on the reservation, too, and they sometimes join the so-called gentle horses, with subversive or amorous intentions. But none of these mustangs were in sight, Martin said; he explained that you can tell them because they are undersized and carry their heads and tails high. We drove into the town of Wadsworth, which is down to three saloons and a general store, and bought some beer. Wadsworth was a humming railroad town until 1905, when the Southern Pacific moved its shops to Sparks, twenty miles nearer Reno. The railroad took its buildings with it on flatcars.

In Wadsworth, we turned left and crossed the Truckee, not more than a hundred feet wide between its ranks of cottonwoods, and struck off onto an old dirt track that ran northward along its east bank. The repossessed lands were on our left, between the road and the river; the first dry irrigation ditch crossed the road not far from the town. We stopped there and looked at the wide fields that had been what McCarran called "little green gems" before the squatters lost them and cut off the water. They were a sedgy prairie, mere rough pasture now. Crested quail ran along the road, and a great blue water snake slid into the ooze that rain had left in the bed of the ditch. It was late October, but winter is always tardy around the lake.

We went on again, losing the river from sight behind its cottonwoods. This is soft, almost wooded country and has little in common either with the bench east of the river between Nixon and Wadsworth or with the desert north of the lake. "We need a storm to drive in the ducks," Martin said. "When they get good flying weather, they don't have to break their flight here." There are no game laws on the reservation. Sometimes the lake can attract a lot of food. To our left were lands repossessed from the Ceresolas, and then lands repossessed from the De Paolis, and then the neat home ranch of Mrs. De Paoli, on a quarter-section that had been duly patented in the sixties and so was hers beyond legal dispute. She is a widow; her husband was old Bill Ceresola's half brother. The De Paolis and the Ceresolas by now were the only two squatter families involved in the wrangle; the Garaventa claim had been ceded to Mrs. De Paoli. Beyond her place, the going got progressively more difficult. We hit a dusty hill the station wagon couldn't climb at first try; we made it two-thirds of the way up, slid halfway back, and charged again. I got out and put sagebrush under the rear wheels; it did little good. But on the tenth or twelfth charge we made the hump.

"This is the Hill Ranch," Martin said. "An Indian is farming it. The river runs through one corner, and the irrigation man from Stewart has rigged a pump to get water on some of the rest." We drove through fields to a square shack with an unroofed porch. From there, we could look down to the river. It was the ranch where the "mean, worthless, and villainous Fleming" had killed Truckee John. A weathered woman in a loose dress was sitting on the porch, peeling potatoes into a bucket; she said her husband was working down by the river. In the summer, he had their two sons, ten and fourteen, to help him, she said, but now they were in school and he had to do the work alone. This family's name was O'Neill. The Paiutes, from the time of the first white settlement in Nevada, took jobs on ranches, and most of them adopted the surnames of the cattle outfits they worked for. There are two or three patronymics of Indian origin on the reservation—Winnemucca and Mauwee, for example—but there are many more names like Dunn, Frazier, and Overton. Nevertheless, nearly all the Indians are full-bloods. Mrs. O'Neill said they were making out pretty well, raising both food crops and hay. The spring floods had washed out their road, but her husband and the boys and her blind brother had restored it, working in water to their waists.

We took leave of Mrs. O'Neill and went back down the road. The Hill Ranch is the most northerly of the repossessed farms. At the southwestern corner of the lands lies the Hoover Ranch, nestling within a curve of the river, and here, too, the Bureau irrigation man had been able to bring water in by pumping. On the way down there, we passed a considerable number of cattle— Bill Ceresola's and the Paiutes', grazing peacefully together. Ceresola's were distinguishable by a long, pendulous strip of skin at the base of the throat—a knife-made dewlap. An Indian named Teddy James, colloquially known as Teddy Jim, was farming the Hoover Ranch, and his home place was more pretentious than the O'Neills'; he had barns and a silo as well as a house. Teddy Jim is a small man who looks like an Eskimo in cowboy boots. His son, a freshman in the agricultural school of the state university, is tall and good-looking. Teddy Jim said he had only thirty-four acres under cultivation, out of a couple of hundred. He raised about fourteen hundred dollars' worth of produce every year, he said, including the hay he fed to his own cattle, and he reckoned it cost the government seven hundred dollars a year to pump water to him. If the Indians got the use of the ditches, he said, the pumping would be unnecessary. Having a common property line with the Ceresolas' home place, he was on a frontier, but he reported that it was a peaceful one. Before the Indians had repossessed the disputed lands, the Ceresolas had been accustomed to gather their cattle along the Truckee for the winter, Teddy Jim said. They had used a hundred acres or so of their own land and fifteen hundred acres of Indian land. Now that the fifteen hundred acres had been repossessed, old Bill Ceresola was concentrating all his cattle—a thousand or fifteen hundred head—on the home ranch, which totalled a hundred and twenty acres. They strayed consistently onto the repossessed lands, through many breaks in the fences; the cottonwood fence posts, installed in 1948, were already rotten. The Tribal Council had not appropriated money to repair the fences, and there was little likelihood that it would. There were no hard words, Teddy Jim told us, although there might be hard feelings. "Old Bill rides down here every couple of days to cuss out the government," he said. "He says he isn't mad at the Paiutes; it's all the government's fault. But he hasn't been down for a week now, because a horse kicked him and broke his leg."

Martin and I drove back to the irrigated delta lands near Nixon, where we sat for a moment looking across the river to the lake. "They say the trout are gone," Martin said, "but I've seen big ones jumping in the evening. They don't run any more, but they're still there." Both river and lake were full of coarse fish, he said, but the Indians had no boats or seines, and no appetite for carp. Afterward, I had tea in Nixon with Brother David, the Episcopalian missionary on the reservation, who in the world of the flesh used to be Gareth Hughes, a silent-movie idol. He has renounced the world but kept his scrapbooks, and it pleased me to know a man who had held in his arms the pulsating forms of the most beautiful women in the world's history, seen by me on the screen of the darkened Nugget Theatre, in Hanover, New Hampshire, between 1920 and 1923. There have been no such women since, but I couldn't bring myself to ask Brother David about them; the cassock intimidated me. Anyway, he showed me their pictures. He spouted Shakespeare, in a musical Welsh voice, and warned me of the machinations of the Mormon Church, which, he said, was laboring to convert the Indians and exploit the untapped mineral resources of all the reservations. He said Abe and Sue, the storekeepers, were Mormon emissaries, and he was so mad at them he wouldn't call at the store for his mail, but had it addressed to Fernley, nineteen miles away. The tea was Lapsang, and he said that later he was going to dine off a buttered parsnip. He invited me to stay, but I pleaded a previous engagement.

Back at the ranch, Harry Drackert told me that he thought I ought to talk to Bill Ceresola and get his side of the question. Harry is friendly with the Indians, but he is friendly with the Ceresolas, too. He is originally out of Pony, Montana, which he ran away from as a youth to follow the rodeo circuit. It is his contention that equities are seldom unmixed, and to illustrate his point he recalled an episode that occurred in a New York speakeasy while he was champion bronc rider of the world. One of his fellow rodeo contenders at Madison Square Garden hit the bartender with a bottle—which he shouldn't have done, Harry freely admits—but then a cop came in and shot the wrong cowboy. "Right is hardly ever all on one side," Harry said, "and as I once heard an old woman say up in the mountains, 'Two heads is better than one, even if one of 'em is a sheepherder.'"

On the following Sunday, Harry and I took the road to Wadsworth, to call on old Bill. The ranch house, a biggish white frame building, as solid and long as a schooner, lay surrounded by tall cottonwood trees and corrals; the place had an air of long-established prosperity. It was evident that lives had gone into making it; it was neither the shiny place of a rich man nor a temporary shelter put up by a homesteader who hopes to develop and sell and get out. We went in through a closed-in porch littered with empty wine gallons and children's playthings (evidence that the Ceresolas had abandoned neither of their ancestral pleasures), and a strapping woman—a daughter or daughter-in-law, I supposed—said she would tell Mr. Ceresola of our arrival. The old man came to meet us, hopping briskly on a crutch, his left leg in a plaster cast, his left arm in a sling. Steel-rimmed spectacles perched on the end of his long Ligurian nose, and he had a fine big sounding box of a chest and big shoulders, which the crutch accentuated as he poled himself along, head down. In the long, wide central room of the ranch house stood a table set for the evening meal of a platoon. Ceresola hopped swiftly in front of us until he got to an easy chair and lowered himself into it, bidding us to take chairs around him. He put the broken leg on a cane chair straight in front of him. Harry began the conversation by asking what had happened to him. We knew he had been kicked by a horse, but the details of such events are of great interest to Harry. Ceresola said he had been riding up a draw behind two mares, in the mountains north of the lake, and was turning his horse to ride around them when one came back and kicked at his horse, or possibly at him, he didn't know which. The kick broke his left leg. The force of the blow made him kick his horse, which jumped, and, what with the pain and all, he slipped to the ground on the left side of the saddle, which left him at the mare's feet. She kicked at him as he was trying to rise—he may have frightened her—and this time she broke his left arm and kicked him above the left kidney, but luckily didn't hit it, he said, for that would have been serious. They had had to haul him off the field in a wagon hitched to a tractor, because the pickup truck couldn't get in across the slews—the marshy spots deep in water.

"How long ago did this happen?" I asked, and he replied, "Nearly two weeks, but I don't feel a hundred per cent yet." He was seventy years old. The bones were mending fine.

After that, we got to talking cattle prices, which were the lowest in the memory of young men, but Ceresola said that in the late winter of 1920–21, when Harding was President, they were even lower. "That winter we sold top February 1st steers for five cents," he said. "And Christmas beef for four and a half, and heifers for four, and when they wanted to buy my old cows for two and a half, I just kicked the animals back on the range. People now don't know what hard times is," he went on, with a grisly satisfaction. When a man won't even agree with you that times are bad, you know he is of an independent and contradictious nature.

After these protocolary preliminaries, I got down to the main purpose of my visit. I asked him how "the case" was going, and he said, "Why, it is the unjustest thing I ever heard of." He went on to assure me that he didn't blame the Indians. "I'm not fighting the Indians," he said. "The Indians don't own the land. The guv-mint owns the land. And I can't fight the guvmint. The Indians naturally want everything they can git for nothing. You can't blame them. And they got an atmosphere that they owned this country and that they can live without working. The older Indi-ans was far better than what they got now, but they ain't the only ones that was. The whites has gone down further. When we came here, we cleared the land with teams. We'd start out with a team in the morning, and at noon we'd put in a fresh team, but *we* was always the same ones. When it was roundup, we'd go out on the range with a pack horse and a bed tarp, but now they want a *cabin* here and a *cabin* there, so they don't have to sleep in th' open. Th' Indians was better then than what the whites is now."

The old man stopped, overcome by emotion, and I took ad-vantage of the pause to ask him when the Ceresolas had come to the place. He said it was in 1900. He himself had been born in Ne-vada, he told me. His father had been brought to Nevada as a little boy by his grandfather; his great-grandfather had led the family's migration. The family had settled in the Carson River Valley. Then, in 1900, Ceresola *père*, with four Nevada-born sons, in-cluding Bill, had moved onto the reservation, buying their land from a man named Ed Short. (Short, I knew, was not one of the original settlers.) "We worked like hell, clearing the land with teams, and now it has gone back to what it was before we showed up here," Ceresola said. "Why, that very land th' Indians has now, the Wingfield bank in Reno give us a mortgage on it, and the Bank of America holds the mortgage now, and I pay interest on it." He got out a blue-bound copy of the Federal Court order that McCarran had referred to—an order known as the Orr Ditch Company Decree, issued in 1926 and allotting water rights along the Truckee. In it the court had allotted water to him and to the De Paolis for land that the government had now returned to the Indians. "We're spoiling them," Ceresola said. "We got them up to creampuffs and ice cream, and now this is what we get. But it ain't the Indians' fault. They take it a damn sight better than if there was a bunch of white people under the same supervision."

When Harry and I got back to his ranch, we found the bar in a bit of a turmoil. It was filled with Indians in their Sunday clothes, carrying feathered headdresses, fringed buckskin suits, and stone-headed war clubs, which they were offering to Joan at sacrifice prices, or even on consignment for sale in her Indian-goods store. The most indignant man there was Martin, but everybody else was pretty mad, too. The Governor's Admission Day committee, Martin explained, had just cut the Indian-parade rates to five dollars a head, for either sex, with no bonuses for horses or papooses. "It makes a fool of me," he said. "I've been going all around the state recruiting, and now it's all off. We've all spent a lot of money on our costumes, and even the fifteen or twenty dollars wouldn't have paid for them. But a fin!"

Levi Frazier's wife, Grace, who is very pretty, said, "Everything turns out this way."

Martin said, "We strike!"

Everybody began to laugh, and Martin's wife, Rosie, who is big and plump, organized a game of Paiute poker.

Indian cowboys at Pyramid Lake. (Creel Collection, courtesy of Special Collections Department, University of Nevada, Reno Library)

Indian cowboys at Pyramid Lake. (Creel Collection, courtesy of Special Collections Department, University of Nevada, Reno Library)

Indian camp at Pyramid Lake, with BIA matron, early-twentieth century. (Courtesy of Nevada Historical Society)

Horses on Smoke Creek Desert, just north of Pyramid Lake. (Gus Bundy Collection, courtesy of Special Collections Department, University of Nevada, Reno Library)

Pelicans on Anaho Island. (Gus Bundy Collection, courtesy of Special Collections Department, University of Nevada, Reno Library)

Joan and Harry Drackert, proprietors of the Sutcliffe Resort at which A. J. Liebling stayed in the 1950s. (Drackert Collection, courtesy of Special Collections Department, University of Nevada, Reno Library)

Resort at Pyramid Lake during the 1920s. The Drackert resort where
Liebling stayed is descended from this complex. (Courtesy of Becky J.
Smith)

The Pyramid. (Gus Bundy Collection, courtesy of Special Collections Department, University of Nevada, Reno Library)

Another view of the Pyramid. (Gus Bundy Collection, courtesy of Special Collections Department, University of Nevada, Reno Library)

The Stone Mother and her basket, a rock formation near the Pyramid. (Gus Bundy Collection, courtesy of Special Collections Department, University of Nevada, Reno Library)

A tufa formation at Pyramid Lake. Tufa is a calcium carbonate, precipitated from lake waters, which covers many rocks surrounding Pyramid Lake in various forms and colors. (Gus Bundy Collection, courtesy of Special Collections Department, University of Nevada, Reno Library)

Rock and pebble formation, Pyramid Lake. (Gus Bundy Collection, courtesy of Special Collections Department, University of Nevada, Reno Library)

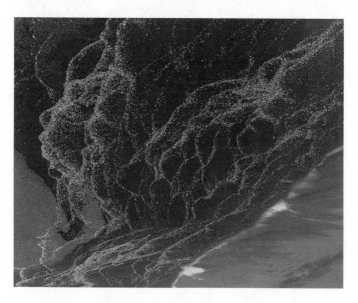

Rows of shells on a black sand beach, Pyramid Lake. (Gus Bundy Collection, courtesy of Special Collections Department, University of Nevada, Reno Library)

4

In 1862, a man named William P. Dole, who was Abraham Lincoln's first Commissioner of Indian Affairs, wrote in his annual report, "However much the fact is to be regretted, it is, nevertheless, almost invariably true that the tracts of land still remaining in the possession of the Indians, small and insignificant as they are when compared with the broad domain of which they were once the undisputed masters, are the objects of the cupidity of their white neighbors; they [the Indians] are regarded as intruders." The attack on the Indian lands took the form of a double envelopment. One wing was composed of people who called themselves friends of the Indians and who initiated a movement to "absorb the Indians" by splitting the reservations into individual allotments and conveying these to individual Indians; such philanthropists argued that the incentive of property ownership would turn the Indians thus favored into hard-working farmers overnight. The result was the General Allotment Act of 1887, which permitted Indians, then almost universally illiterate, to claim, own, lease, mortgage, and sell their personal portions of the tribal heritage. At the time the act was passed, approximately two hundred and fifty thousand Indians held a hundred and thirty-eight million acres. In 1934, when Congress ended the allotment system, there were about fifty thousand more Indians in the United States, but they had only forty-eight million acres left; what had been absorbed was the acreage. The other wing of the envelopment was made up of less patient whites, who simply moved onto reservations and squatted there. It was in Dole's term of office that the first squatters—or settlers, as they are sometimes more charitably called—moved onto the Paiute reservation that surrounds Pyramid Lake, a little more than thirty miles north of Reno, Nevada, and it was not until 1936 that the United States government began taking any effective steps to get them—or, rather, what lawyers call their "successors in interest"—off the twenty-one hundred acres they had taken over.

The Pyramid Lake band of Paiutes, known of old as the Cuyui-dokado, the Eaters of the Cui-Ui, a fish uniquely indigenous to that lake, came near losing the twenty-one hundred acres for good in 1924. In that year, under Calvin Coolidge (whose picture taken in an Indian war bonnet was his only gesture of friendship to the red man), Congress passed a bill authorizing the squatters to buy the land they had appropriated at a cut-rate price, but the squatters, after making a first payment, defaulted. Twelve years passed, and then, when the Department of the Interior at length moved to put the squatters off, the late Senator Patrick A. McCarran, of Nevada, offered a bill to give them the land with no further payment, or, failing that, to sell it to them at bargain-basement rates. The bill did not pass. He offered bills to the same effect and with the same result at each successive Congress until 1953. Meanwhile, the government had instituted suits to oust the squatters, had successfully carried them through the Circuit Court of Appeals, and, in 1944, had beaten back an appeal to the Supreme Court. In 1948, the Indians, by court order, reëntered into possession of the disputed land. None of this, however, deterred McCarran from offering his bills.

The land in question included six hundred irrigated acres along the Truckee River—exceedingly valuable in that region of sparse pasture. But in 1948, when the Paiutes moved back in, they found these acres dry as a bone, because the settlers, who still legally owned adjacent property, claimed ditch and water rights and had cut the water off. So the parties in opposition remained—the Indians with the waterless land and the settlers annually allowing several million gallons of water that was theirs by nominal title to run down into Pyramid Lake. When I first became aware of this situation, it struck me, in my Eastern ignorance, as about the most implausible one I had ever come across, but investigation disclosed that the setup was warranted sound Nevada law by Senator McCarran. The Senator apparently imposed his views on the government attorneys, since they brought no action to get the water for the Indians.

My own interest in the struggle at Pyramid Lake began gradually—almost accidentally—while I was out there in the summer of 1949, waiting for the legal mills to grind in Reno. But by the fall of 1953, my interest—grown to the point of absorption—took me back to Nevada with a copy of the late Felix S. Cohen's "Handbook of Federal Indian Law," a sheaf of transcripts of the hearings on McCarran bills of various vintages, and a book on the northern Paiutes in my suitcase. Even if I had been indifferent to the principals, the struggle would have had for me the odd fascination of an honest wrestling match—a spectacle so rare that few men now alive can boast of having seen one. I once witnessed one in the old Hippodrome, between two wrestlers whose employers had failed to conclude a trade agreement. It lasted three hours and a half, and nothing happened; both men simply shoved as hard as they could. It had the charm of the incredible; I have wondered ever since what would have ultimately occurred if the promoters, with an eye on the lighting bill, had not stopped it. The Hippodrome had fallen on lean days, and there were sometimes long lapses between attractions. Would the wrestlers' skeletons have been found, leaning against each other like skeletons of horn-locked stags, when the Hippodrome's opera company opened its season a few months later? Or would the gladiators have simply quit for breakfast? The outcome of the wrestlers' battle meant nothing to me, but in the Pyramid Lake case I liked the Paiutes, and although I had never met Senator McCarran, I didn't think I would care for him.

Nothing had changed at the lake between my two visits. Upon my return there, I talked with the cui-ui eaters, who said, in their Amerindian idiom, so fraught with the sombre dignity of a vanishing race, that they were "stuck until old Pat conked out," and with seventy-year-old Bill Ceresola, the peppery patriarch of the squatters, who said that the eviction from the Indian lands was the unjustest thing he'd ever heard of. The adversaries appeared equally immovable and equally prolific, with successors in interest already begotten, and ready to beget new successors in interest, and so on, *ad infinitum*. Of the five squatters originally embroiled in the dispute only two were still left in contention— Bill Ceresola and his sister-in-law, Mrs. M. P. De Paoli. The others had ceded their claims and rights to these two. Ceresola was living in his ranch house on a tract of a hundred and twenty acres that belonged to him without legal dispute, and Mrs. De Paoli was occupying her hundred and sixty acres of patent lands, and the repossessed, dried-out Indian land was all around them.

From Pyramid Lake, I went on to Reno to inquire into the water rights law and to seek an interview with Senator McCarran. He was no harder to find than the Archbishop in Rennes. When I checked in at the Hotel Riverside on my return from the lake, the public-address system was paging the Senator in both bars, the gambling casino, the Chuck-Wagon Restaurant, and the lobby— "Senator McCarran is wanted on the long-distance telephone." This sound, repeated throughout the day like the note of an Ambrose Channel whistling buoy, indicated that the Senator was in residence and on the hoof. It was interspersed with jingling announcements of jackpots on slot machines. Later in the evening, when the Senator had presumably retired to his apartment, the calls to the telephone ceased, but the slot machines went on all night.

The first back I recognized at the Riverside's corner bar belonged to my 1949 counsel, familiarly known as the Judge. All Nevada lawyers over the age of thirty-five have been judges at one time or another, and "Judge" is the courteous form of address, like "Captain" on a fishing dock. My Judge had been on the bench in White Pine County; I called him my White Pine Blackstone. His back was broad, and tailored with an elegance that advertised prosperity. At the sound of my voice, he turned with a smile of friendly commiseration. I hastily assured him that my marital situation was without flaw. If he was disappointed, he concealed it handsomely. He had no more need of divorce clients, he told me. He bought me a drink, and said his affluence, which he freely acknowledged, derived from his appointment as a Special Master in Bankruptcy for a race track at Las Vegas, whose promoters had forgotten that you need more customers for such an enterprise than for a craps table. "Also, all the potential customers in the vicinity were *at* craps tables," the Judge said. "The track stands as a monument to the failure of a gambling community to figure percentages. Dust and wind, like everything in Las Vegas."

I tried to sound the Judge out on Senator McCarran and his view of the water laws, but homicide is the branch of practice by which the White Pine Blackstone grades attorneys. "Pat McCarran is a fine criminal lawyer," he said. "If I ever defended myself overeffectively with a deadly weapon placed in my grasp by hazard at a moment when I was temporarily out of my mind, there is no one I would be prouder to have in my corner. I will never forget Pat's defense of a Chinese prostitute named Hazel Wan, who punctured her pimp with a penknife. Pat told the jury that if the wounds had been treated properly at the hospital the man would have survived. He implied that they were trifling evidences of an overdemonstrative woman's affection. 'Will you blight the life of this broken reed?' he asked the jurors. They acquitted her and she went back to work. Prostitution was legal here then."

I wanted to get a variety of opinions on the water laws before talking to Senator McCarran, and I began by telephoning Judge E. P. Carville. Carville, too, had been a judge—in Elko, which is a cattle town—before moving to the metropolis. A Democrat, he had also been Governor of the state and, immediately thereafter, a United States Senator, filling out the term of James G. Scrugham, who died in 1945. But he had been beaten in the Democratic primary in 1946, a result generally attributed to the machinations of McCarran. The Democrat who beat Carville, an undertaker named Berkeley Bunker—"a fine figure of a man walking in front of a casket," his admirers called him—had, in turn, gone down to defeat in the election, a result generally attributed to the split in the Party. I knew Carville by reputation as a quiet, accomplished lawyer, who was familiar with the Pyramid Lake case because, in company with James E. Curry, a Washington attorney, he had been retained by the Paiutes in 1949 as counsel for the tribe. This step had been dictated by a number of changes in Washington. The Interior Department's Bureau of Indian Affairs suffered a loss in fighting edge after the resignation of John Collier as Commissioner in 1945, followed by that of

Harold L. Ickes as Secretary of the Interior a year later. Even more important, however, was the change in the Department of Justice, on which Senator McCarran, after the departure of the last Roosevelt Attorney General, exercised a paralyzing influence as Chairman of the Senate Judiciary Committee. Representatives of the Department of the Interior appeared against each McCarran land-grab bill, but they could take only defensive action, and Justice, which must represent the government in all legal disputes, tamely acceded to the Alice in Wonderland doctrine that a man could own ditches on land the highest court had ruled was never his. The Paiutes, therefore, were obliged to find someone to champion their cause, and retained Curry and Judge Carville on their own. Curry, a most aggressive fellow, favored direct action. "The government failing in its duty," he declared, "they [the Paiutes] have the right to retake possession of their own property, including the necessary ditches." McCarran, who had been the Paiutes' chief opponent before Congress, forthwith felt impelled to protect them from Curry. Speaking in the Senate as an old Indian-lover, he accused the lawyer of trying to exploit the Paiutes. The Indian Bureau then eliminated Curry by forbidding the tribe to pay him any fees. When McCarran had established the principle that the Indians might have no representation outside the Department of Justice (which he could stop from representing them), he went back to his adversary position. Carville's interest in the case was passive; if Curry had brought legal action, he would have counselled him on Nevada law, but when Curry dropped out, the Judge felt obliged to do the same, and tranquilly continued with the rest of his excellent practice. (He obtained a divorce last summer for Bobo Rockefeller, which gives one a rough idea of his standing in Reno's nobility of the robe.)

I made an appointment with Carville, but not for a very early hour. Reno is a city in which it is foolish to be in a hurry. Walking too briskly to a rendezvous, one may pass up a slot machine that is on the point of yielding a hundred and fifty silver dollars. (If a machine does not respond to your first coin, however, it is no use insisting. Chalk up your lost dollar to mistaken intuition, and try to sharpen your sensitivity.) Or your favorite number may be preparing to run on the wheel at the Bank Club, on Center Street, which has no double zero. The percentage against you there is only half as bad as on the other wheels in town; even if you lose, it is a bargain. One thing you are sure of missing if you do not procrastinate is good conversation. The woman who runs the book department at Armanko's store, for example, is the widow of a man who for fourteen years ran the horse book at the Bank. She herself worked in the accounting department there, and likes to talk about an old gambler called Pop, who had made her the guardian of his burning-money. "Pop always wanted to be cremated," she says. "And no matter how old he got, he also always had something going for him in the future book on the Kentucky Derby. That way, whether he lived or died, he had something to look forward to." There is no such talk to be had at Brentano's.

Leaving the Riverside, I tacked down Virginia Street as far as Douglas Alley;—at which point I was eight dollars ahead— walked through the Nevada Turf Club, and came out on Commercial Row, a one-sided street that runs beside the railroad tracks. There I entered the Wine House, a restaurant with a painted ceiling—all cupids, like the *plafond* of a municipal theatre in a small French city. The Wine House menu offers kippered Alaskan cod, Pacific Coast *langouste*, Coo-Coo clams, colored grain-fed chicken (the boss believes white birds have no flavor), ham hocks and beans, mountain-brook trout, *manteca* beef (a poetic exaggeration), and mulligan stew. It also offers a slug of bonded bourbon for thirty-five cents. On the walls are hand paintings of Cleopatra with a slave girl and a parrot, of Jim Butler and his donkey discovering the great silver lode at Tonopah in 1900, and of the Battle of the Marianas; there is also a painting called "The Love Song" (a fat man playing a mandolin to his girl; A. Zoppi, Florence, Italy, artist); one called "The Girl of Kosovo, 1389" (this refers to the date of the battle, not the painting); and one called "The Happy Family" (gamin on swing, indulgent grandfather, beaming mother), on which Mr. Frankovitch, the proprietor, is particularly high. "That's a picture that can go in any company," he told me.

I lunched beatifically and then started back up Center Street, which parallels Virginia; paused at the one-zero table, where I built up a lead of a hundred and twenty-five dollars but blew it; and still got to the First National Bank Building in plenty of time for my appointment with Judge Carville. As a matter of fact, I also made a detour to Lake Street and stopped by the Santa Fe Hotel, a Basque *pension* patronized by sheepherders, who, like lighthouse keepers, take occasional sabbaticals from solitude. McCarran, while throttling immigration from most parts of Europe, had a habit of introducing a special bill every couple of years to admit to the country from three to five hundred Basque sheepherders, in addition to the normal Spanish quota, on the ground that they were needed to save the American wool industry. These bills invariably passed. The reason the supply of Basques must be continually renewed is that after being in this country for a while they go to work in restaurants. A Breton *chef de cuisine* told me, while we were having a Pernod at the Santa Fe bar, that he had three Basques in his kitchen crew at a restaurant called Eugene's. Some of the Nevada Basques are from the French side of the border and others from the Spanish, but they have *une langue à eux,* the chef informed me, in which they can communicate. He said that when he wished to discourage his helpers from talking Basque exclusively, which he considered unchummy, he addressed them in Breton. This served to show them they had no *monopole des mystères.* There was a legend that for Western sheep ranchers who disliked a labor turnover Basques of a less volatile grade were available. These, so the story went, were flown without visas from Spain to Havana and from Havana to an airfield near Salt Lake City, where they were delivered to their employers. If they then tried to become *sauciers,* their bosses turned them in to the Immigration agents. If, however, an Immigration man picked one up in the course of a routine investigation—perhaps on the tip of a jealous husband—the employer enlisted a member of Congress to bring in an individual-hardship bill legitimizing the peon's stay.

When at last I reached Mr. Carville's office, the old Judge— Notre Dame, class of 1909—said he had no doubt the Indians could get the water that had been allotted to the land in question by the United States District Court in 1926 (when the squatters still held it); he also thought they could get the right to use the ditches on what was now their property. To do so, though, they would have to commence new litigation. Under Nevada law, the Judge said, the owner of a water right has the privilege of transferring his decreed water to other lands, if he has such lands, but if he fails for several years to transfer it, his right lapses. There might be some question as to precisely how many years it would take for a right to lapse, but he thought three years would be sufficient. Five years had passed since the Indians had repossessed the lands, and so any continued claim to the water by the dispossessed squatters was pretty tenuous. "I told the Tribal Council that a long time ago," the Judge said. "But they didn't want to spend the money to commence a court action, or maybe they didn't have it. I don't know." In any event, the Judge felt that with each passing year the Paiutes' chances in such an action improved. We chatted a bit about politics, and he said that between July, 1945, when he was appointed to the Senate, and December, 1946, when he got through there, Senator McCarran had never once spoken to him. "He is neither a Democrat nor a Republican," he said. "Just a McCarrancrat."

From Judge Carville's office I went to the office of Sidney Robinson, the attorney for Bill Ceresola, the squatter patriarch, and for Mrs. De Paoli. Robinson, a tall, busy, genial man, gave me an excellent map of the litigated lands and ditches along with a copy of the brief he had filed with the United States Supreme Court in 1943 supporting a petition for a writ of certiorari, which meant a request for the Court to review the decision of the Circuit Court of Appeals against his clients. The petition had been turned down. The Indians might win a suit for water rights, Mr. Robinson admitted, but he hoped that the whole question was about to become academic; Senator McCarran and the settlers were even now trying to agree on a price that the Senator might, with some expectation of success, propose to the Department of the Interior with the idea of buying the settlers out— patent lands, buildings, improvements, claims, and all. This was something McCarran had said in 1949 he would never consent to, but, like the Merrimac in the battle with the Monitor, he was backing off. "If they can get together," Mr. Robinson said, "and if the Senator can get together with the Department. . . ." He smiled, and held out his hands with the palms up.

I returned to the Riverside, and since the muezzin at the microphone was not calling for Senator McCarran, I asked the handsome young woman at the desk whether the Senator was in his suite or making a parochial visit. She said he was in, so I went up to my room and telephoned him to ask for an appointment. The Senator answered the phone himself; his voice was not oratorical, as I had imagined it would be, but dry, irascible, and tired. He expected hostility, and until recently he had courted it, but in his seventy-eighth year he was trying to create the image of a lovable McCarran. He could not re-create one, because it had never existed; even when he was a boy at school, old-timers said, his classmates refused to play marbles with him, because he made up his own rules. By openly opposing the election of Tom Mechling, the Democratic candidate for junior senator from Nevada in 1952, he had further split the Party in the state; Mechling was beaten by George (Molly) Malone. Now McCarran was desperately anxious to put the Party together again before he himself should have to stand for renomination, in 1956. By getting Mechling beaten, the old man had cost his Party control of the Senate. With Mechling, the Democrats would have numbered forty-eight, as against forty-seven Republicans and an independent. It was unlikely that McCarran had foreseen this result—more probably he had expected a Republican landslide—but it had made him as unpopular in the national Party, even among Dixiecrats as he already was in Nevada. To present the new, benevolent McCarran to his constituents, a group of his friends had bought a small weekly newspaper, the *Nevada State News,* which at the time of my visit was publishing a vitaminized biography of McCarran the statesman. I had read one installment of it over my Coo-Coo clams at the Wine House. "The careers of few Americans indeed can produce as many high spots" was a sample sentence.

When McCarran heard that all I wanted to know about was the Indian story, he said, "Why don't you ask some disinterested party?" I enumerated the people I had already talked to, and said it would be impossible to get a clear picture of the case without him; it would be like a highball without whiskey. He said he was very busy—this was coquetry, I was sure—but would meet me downstairs in the Chuck-Wagon Restaurant at nine o'clock the next morning.

That evening, upon entering the hotel's casino for my apéritif—a Scotch-and-soda and twenty dollars' worth of twenty-five-cent chips—I saw the Senator there. Seated at the entrance to the Chuck-Wagon, which is a bay of the casino furnished with banquettes and dining tables, he commanded a fine view of gambling and gastronomy alike, while gamblers and diners commanded a fine view of him. I put a quarter chip on zero and watched him between plays. There he sat, unmistakable under his halo of white hair, with his noble face an old-rose glow above his blue serge double-breasted jacket. Around him sat a number of men I had had drinks with at one time or another—real-estate operators, cattlemen, and gamblers. They sat "like Indians around a fire, each with his good meat and drink"—to borrow a simile from Colonel John R. Stingo, an old mining-promoter friend of mine. The Senator's complexion heightened the simile; his hair represented the smoke. Because of my appointment with him for the next day, I felt it would be gauche to enter the circle at this time, particularly since he had said he was hard at work. On the other hand, it was useless to pretend I did not see him; it would have been like pretending not to notice Louis XIV at Versailles. As I studied him, I saw that he had a fine, witty face, like that of a John Barrymore grown old—a Roman profile half buried in suet. Newspaper photographs coarsen most subjects, and in the case of such a man as McCarran, they sometimes induce a dangerous contempt. I had thought of him as a beefy ward-heeler type, but now I perceived that he was really a beautiful old rogue, with a mobile, calculating mask.

When the customary call droned through the room—"Senator McCarran is wanted on the long-distance telephone"—he at first pretended to take no notice. After the sixth or eighth repetition, he rose, having by that time made it apparent that he hurried at no man's bidding, and solemnly swept toward the lobby, pushing his jacket buttons well in advance of his chin. When he returned, he was preceded by Mrs. McCarran, a substantial matron in evening dress, who looked rather like Tenniel's Red Queen. She is a great Bingo player. The McCarrans paused benevolently at one of the craps tables—the Senator once testified that the economy of Nevada rested on gambling—and I could see he was pleased with the amount of action. (After we got to know each other, he would stop at a roulette table if he saw me playing and give me an encouraging pat on the shoulder.) As I watched the McCarrans, Mert Wertheimer, one of the two brothers who operate the casino (they are émigrés from Detroit), said to me, "There goes what I call a statesman. Shoots his limit of duck and partridge every season, too." A slight cloud passed over Mert's face, and, following the direction of his glance, I saw a uniformed Reno cop who had stopped by for a snort. "I've been in this state ten years and I still feel nervous when I see one of those guys in my joint," Mr. Wertheimer said. "It's wonderful to know they can't put the shake on you." Zero came up, but all I had on it was my last quarter, and it didn't repeat. I went down the street to try my luck at the Bank Club.

When I entered the Chuck-Wagon Restaurant at eight-thirty the next morning, McCarran was at his table, surrounded by barber-shaved toffs in dark glasses and Pendleton shirts—the morning uniform of the man-about-Reno. For all I knew he had been there all night, because the casino never closes, but he looked too fresh and rosy. I took a table by myself and had breakfast. By the headlines in the morning paper—the *Nevada State Journal*—I saw that the United States had concluded a deal for the use of airfields in Spain, whither McCarran had already channeled almost a quarter of a billion dollars. I was downing my second cup of coffee when the Senator rose and, with a fatherly smile, approached my table; some of our mutual acquaintances had probably identified me the previous evening. He waved me down when I started to stand up, and, seating himself opposite me, he began, "Perhaps it will do no harm if I go into a little of the history of this case." Here he fixed his honest blue eyes on mine, just as the fellow who sold me a combination lawnmower sharpener and glass cutter at the special price of one dollar at the Delaware County Fair, in Ohio, had done only a month or so previously. "The Paiute is not an agrarian Indian," he began. I nodded, and he said, "I am glad you understand that. The Easterner is often so easily imposed upon—so credulous." I remembered just in time that the glass cutter had taken a good-sized hunk out of my lawnmower blade.

"My father came across the plains as a soldier under the command of Major General Winfield Scott Hancock," the Senator went on. "So I feel well acquainted with the subject. He went to California and took his discharge, and he came back here in the Civil War, with the First California Volunteers. After the war, soldiers from Fort Churchill left the Army and took up land. They went up to the Big Bend of the Truckee River. They took up the land at a dollar an acre—twenty-five cents down and twenty years to pay the rest. Oxen were the means of transportation."

"Wasn't that on a reservation?" I asked.

The Senator waved me down. "I'll get to that in just a minute," he said. "The railroad—the Central Pacific Railroad, as it was then—was approaching the little town of Wadsworth. It set up its shops there. The settlers raised crops to sell. They raised the hay they called Blue John, and they got a hundred to a hundred and fifty dollars a ton. The Indians were glad to have them there. Then, in 1874, President Grant issued an executive order proclaiming a reservation. There the settlers were, with their beautiful little green gems of alfalfa, like emerald isles, all glistening by the bank of the Truckee, and they had been forced into trespass."

"But I thought the courts ruled that the reservation dated from 1859," I said, expressing with a timid smile my reluctance to question his statement.

"There is a contention to that effect," the Senator said. "But it is untenable." He then raced smoothly through the talks on Pyramid Lake he had delivered before Congressional committees in 1937, 1943, and 1949—the transcripts of which I had in my suitcase upstairs—slightly amending his text only when he got to the part about how the settlers would have liked to pay up in 1932 but couldn't. "There were fourteen banks in the State of Nevada," he said. "They closed their doors, never to open again. There was an exception. There was one little bank, but they wouldn't lend you a dollar on your right eye. You had to put two eyes on the table." The way I remembered that passage was "You could not borrow a dollar on a twenty-dollar gold piece."

"The strangest part about it is that what they called the reservation now never was a reservation at all," McCarran said, and when I looked surprised, he explained, "They claim to have lost the original map. I asked the Department of the Interior for that map a hundred times, and they just grinned at me. The high land on the Truckee River marked the intended boundary between the Italian farms at Wadsworth and the Indian lands at Nixon. But it is no longer susceptible of proof."

I asked the Senator what in his opinion had started the row, since the Indians had apparently accepted the settlers' presence for so many years. "There was a woman Indian Superintendent—a Miss Alida Bowler—here in the first years of the Roosevelt administration," he said, and he gave me the glass-cutter pitchman's look again, deep into both pupils, with dignified sincerity. "I'm not saying she had Leftist tendencies, or anything," he continued. "But these Paiutes turned up at hearings in Washington using the expression 'minority group.'"

"Well?" I asked.

"They were stimulated," the Senator said. "And it isn't that I don't like Indians." This reminded me of old Bill Ceresola, who had told me that he liked Indians, too. Amusement convulsed the Senator's thespian eyebrows, and he chuckled. "I remember a neighbor we had when I was a boy," he said. "Old Charlie Beecroft, a white sheep rancher. He married a squaw and recognized her son. When the son grew up, he sent him to college, and when old Charlie died, he left him the ranch. The son married a white woman. He was a fine fellow. But my mother never could stand the idea. She once asked the young Mrs. Beecroft, 'Tell me, is he as black under his shirt as he is in his face?'" The Senator threw back his milkweed mane and laughed. Then an expression of seriousness—almost sorrow—formed a film over his ingenuous merriment. "It was a splendid ranch," he said, "but young Beecroft lost it. He drank." The Senator looked over my shoulder at the long bar behind me, which was doing a mild morning business in whiskey sours and Bloody Marys. "He gambled," he said, and turned a horrified gaze upon the foundations of Nevada's economy, where the ivory ball was circling its track languidly, like a race horse having a morning breeze.

A woebegone-looking man wearing a soiled, dry raincoat buttoned to his neck, and with a mustache as dirty as a tobacco-chewer's toothbrush, rushed up to McCarran with an opened newspaper and, pointing to the headline about the airfields, shouted, "So happy, Senator! I'm so happy!" I learned afterward that he was on the staff of the *Nevada State News*—McCarran's cheerleader. McCarran waved him away.

The Senator's talks on Pyramid Lake, I knew from my reading of the Congressional hearings, usually ran to around twenty-two and a half pages, and since I could see that he was following the traditional script, I attempted to halt him at about page 10. "Senator," I said, "do you think the bill you have in Congress now has any chance to pass?"

To my astonishment, he stopped as easily as a well-broken hackamore horse. "I've given up," he said.

"It's the first decision I've ever heard of you losing," I said, and he replied, after a nod and a wave of acknowledgment, "You can't win 'em all."

What he was after now, he said, was to induce the government to buy the De Paoli and Ceresola patent lands, with the improvements and what he called their "unchallenged" water rights. Mrs. De Paoli was being reasonable, he said, but Ceresola was holding out for a price that even McCarran didn't think he could get the Department of the Interior to approve. "He wants two hundred thousand," he said. I recalled that the Senator's bills would have authorized the settlers to buy the twenty-one hundred Indian acres, including six hundred under irrigation, for twenty-two thousand dollars, plus interest—perhaps thirty thousand dollars in all. Ceresola had a hundred and twenty patented acres, ninety-five of them irrigated. "I think I could get him a pretty good figure, but he's stubborn," the Senator said.

When I heard McCarran say he'd given up, I felt it was a historic moment. After all, he had started with this case during his first term in the Senate, where he had arrived on Franklin D. Roosevelt's shiny new band wagon ("A New Deal for America: Roosevelt, Garner, and McCarran"). In 1937, he had introduced his first bill to override the action by which the Secretary of the Interior terminated the squatters' tenure, and, after his bill failed, he had attempted to cultivate the uncultivatable Ickes. In 1938, Ickes was engaged in a struggle to obtain the confirmation of an assistant secretary named Burlew; McCarran went over to Ickes' side, asking him to reciprocate by dropping the litigation against the squatters. Ickes accepted the support, and continued to oppose McCarran by throwing his weight against the Indian bills the Senator tossed into the hopper in 1939 and 1941. But Burlew himself tried to reciprocate on at least one occasion. In 1941, while Collier, then the Indian Commissioner, was on an inspection trip in Arizona—about as far from Washington as a man can well get in the continental United States—McCarran had a colleague call a spot meeting of the Senate Committee on Indian Affairs, at which Burlew informed the members that Interior had changed its position and now favored the Pyramid Lake Bill. Collier, warned by a telegram—or perhaps by signal fires—flew back to Washington to contradict his fellow-official. Ickes backed Collier. Lying on a hillside on Block Island and looking out over the Atlantic, Collier told me about all this in the summer of 1953. A small, leathery man with an understated, astringent humor, Collier had remained in Indian work as professor of anthropology at the College of the City of New York. McCarran, I knew, had approached Ickes again in 1941, after a United States District Court in Nevada had ruled in favor of the settlers. This time, he wanted the Secretary to promise not to appeal the court's decision. Ickes turned him down, and the government won the appeal. In 1943, in 1945, and in each succeeding Congress, the Senator presented his bills as automatically as he accumulated seniority, and he

114

fought for them as hard as if they had involved Pan American Airways, or Chiang Kai-shek, or General Franco, or Stanley Dollar, of the American President Lines—all of them, like the squatters, among his protégés. In 1950, for example, an aggressive Indian Superintendent named E. Reeseman Fryer began a survey of the possibility of putting in a duplicate irrigation system, which would make the disputed ditches superfluous. McCarran terrified the Indian Commissioner into transferring Fryer. The Pyramid Lake case was by that time a *cause célèbre* in Indian affairs, and the National Congress of American Indians protested the transfer to President Truman, who personally quashed it. McCarran was not done, however. Four months later, Fryer received an offer of a much better appointment in the Technical Coöperation Administration. He accepted. McCarran was a member of the Appropriations Committee, and the T.C.A. was short of money.

This was a small part of what I knew about the background of the Paiute case, and what I knew was a very small part of all that had happened. So when I heard the old boy say he had quit, I felt as if I were witnessing the withdrawal of the Roman legions from Britain—the first backward step of an empire. The Riverside—that warm, reassuring recess of Reno in which the Senator held court when he was home from Washington—was no longer a political scale model of the rest of Nevada, and he knew it. Down in Clark County, which includes Las Vegas and the even younger industrial town of Henderson, there was a new group of voters, for whom he had never done favors, and the population there was growing faster than it was in the Truckee and Carson River garden patch, which up to 1945 had held more than half the voters in Nevada. Most of the southerners, being newcomers to the state, were unimpressed by the Senator's old-style frontier foofaraw. And in his own province his vindictiveness had alienated at least a third of his fellow-Democrats. He had too often violated the commandment to go easy on the fellows you beat, because you may need them next year. Even the Nevada press was no longer solidly his. Some years before, when an insignificant weekly called the *Nevada State News* criticized him, he had been influential enough to induce its advertisers to boycott it, causing the editor to complain later, "I felt like a whore without a kimono." (This was the paper that McCarran's friends bought, at a knockdown price.) But now there was a strong, crudely violent opposition paper in Las Vegas, the *Sun*, which was even reaching newsstands in Reno. And when McCarran tried the same tactics against it, he failed. The old man's heart, which had nearly given out late in 1951, was functioning passably well, but the fear of another attack must have been with him, along with other fears more poignant. The grandeur to which he had grown accustomed late in life hung on his success in wheedling votes from ditch riders and cocktail waitresses. Getting elected in Nevada is small retail business.

Perhaps to prove how good his health was, the Senator showed me large, glossy photographic scenes of a goose hunt he had been on with a fellow Senator, Cordon, of Oregon—a Republican, of course. There the statesmen stood, like ritual butchers among the slaughtered poultry. But he had no more strength for his war with the Paiutes.

Although Pyramid Lake is only thirty miles or so from Reno, when I returned to it after my talk with McCarran it seemed far more remote—as remote as the Late Stone Age from the Late Nylon-Chromium-Plastic. There it lay, coldly beautiful in early November, between the savage *djebels* of the Lake and Virginia ranges. At the Pyramid Lake Guest Ranch, run by Harry and Joan Drackert, I found that the last divorcée of the year had departed. Bolivar, the Drackerts' old shepherd dog, wandered among the deserted cabins, mistily remembering the summer's handouts. In a corral at the top of the hillside pasture, Andy K., Harry's thoroughbred stallion, looked over the bars with distaste at his owner's battered mares—good blood, but long in the tooth and holding no surprises. (The fashionable imported Irish and English studs, who hold court in California, get their pick of the sweet young things. For an old stallion, Nevada is an Elba.) In the bar, I found two or three Paiutes, together with some Mexican section hands from the branch line of the Southern Pacific that runs behind the ranch and a couple of mustangers who had been collecting wild horses for a dog-meat cannery. Four months earlier, Congress had passed a bill allowing Indians to buy hard liquor for the first time in over a hundred years, but the Paiutes were still faithful to pop. When the Indians heard my news about the Senator, they were not jubilant, as I had expected them to be.

"We still see plenty of buck," a brave with a Coke said. "They pass the buck for nearly hundred years already about those lands."

Still, it was a victory, a 7-Up drinker pointed out. "Miss Bowler would like to hear about it," he said, and smiled. "It was really she who started us to fight."

Miss Bowler, I knew, had retired from the Indian Service and was living in Glendale, a suburb of Los Angeles. Since I wanted to go to Las Vegas before I returned East, I decided to make it a three-cornered flight—Reno to Los Angeles to Las Vegas. This would enable me to stop and see her on the way, and it wouldn't add much to the total distance, as people reckon such things in that corner of the world.

My plane landed at the Los Angeles International Airport, and from there I travelled, by bus and taxi, through twenty-five miles of identical, vaguely familiar streets of flimsy, undifferentiated one-family houses. I wondered what made them seem familiar, since I had never been there before, and then I remembered the silent films of my extreme youth, with the Keystone Cops chasing Snub Pollard down identical vistas. Midway, I passed the clump of skyscrapers from whose windows Al St. John and Harold Lloyd used to dangle in their acrobatic comedy bits. My heart rose to my throat as I looked up, but they were no longer there. In a couple of minutes, I was again among the serried *isbas,* which became fresher and newer as I went along, with lawns of double-bed instead of twin-bed size. These were the bungalows where young one-reeler husbands, returning unexpectedly because they had forgotten their valises, used to find miraculous comics flirting with their wives. The wives, displaying alarm by throwing up their hands and rolling their eyes (Subtitle: "My husband!"), would shove the comics through windows, where they would get stuck and dogs would bite them. It was a sentimental journey into the past, and when I rang Miss Bowler's doorbell, I half expected a bucket of wallpaper paste to fall on me as the door opened.

Nothing like that happened. Miss Bowler, who has bobbed white hair and a round pink face, turned out to be a decisive, informal lady of the sort I used to associate with the Federal Theatre and Writers' Projects. She was, in her way, almost as great an anachronism as a Mack Sennett girl, but she recalled the hopeful, energetic prime of Mrs. Roosevelt and Frances Perkins. I told her that until I became interested in the Paiutes I had never heard of a woman Indian Superintendent, and she said that she was the first ever appointed. In the twenties, she had served for five years as California secretary of the American Indian Defense Association, she said; Collier had been its national executive secretary. She had quit that job to become public-relations director of the Los Angeles police force. When President Roosevelt appointed Collier Indian Commissioner, Collier had asked her to join the Indian Bureau. She had consented on condition that she be allowed to work in the field instead of in an office in Washington, and had been appointed to the superintendency of the Carson Indian Agency, which includes a couple of California reservations as well as all the reservations in Nevada. (The Indians on the California reservations are mostly Paiutes, too.) She had first heard of the land dispute at Pyramid Lake when she visited the reservation there during her initial tour of the region under her jurisdiction. It had seemed to her intolerable that the Indians should have been deprived of the use of their lands over a period of seventy-five years, without a nickel of compensation. The Indians had laughed and dared her to try to do something about it. "Being a woman, I imagine I felt under a greater obligation to show them," she told me.

Miss Bowler went on to say that she had gathered all the information she could about the history of the dispute, not only from records but from witnesses. There were still Indians living then who remembered how an Indian named Truckee John had been murdered for his land by the squatters' predecessors in interest. She had jabbed the Indian Bureau—and, through the Bureau, the

Department of the Interior, and, through Interior, the Department of Justice—into action in behalf of her Paiutes, made skeptical by history. During the five years she served as the superintendent at Stewart, she said, the squatters at Pyramid Lake took an average of eight thousand dollars' worth of crops annually off the disputed lands, and Heaven knows what they had taken during the previous seventy-odd years and during the ten years that followed before the Indians regained possession. "Who will ever pay for that?" she asked with spirit, just as if she still expected something to be done to compensate the Indians. I could see why the old Senator had never liked her. She told me that he had finally prevailed upon the Indian Bureau, even while Collier was still in charge, to transfer her out, because she was "prejudiced." "As if you could be too prejudiced in favor of the people it is your duty to protect!" she said. "It is like a policeman being prejudiced in favor of the law." It was not too difficult to understand how the transfer had been brought about—Ickes still hoping he could get McCarran to work with him on other issues, McCarran reminding him of how he had helped get Burlew appointed, the argument that the Bowler transfer would remove an irritant without weakening the Department's stand on the main issue. Miss Bowler probably understood, too, by now. She had resigned from the Indian Bureau a few months later, she said, but had returned to it, and had not retired finally until 1952.

After the transfer of Miss Bowler, the Pyramid Lake case that she had tackled so briskly and hopefully dragged on—through the brisk, hopeful early years of the New Deal, the recession of 1938, the Ethiopian War, the Franco rebellion in Spain, the fight over increasing the number of Supreme Court justices (in which McCarran had favored an increase to eleven, including him), Munich, the Anschluss, the career of Joe Louis, miniature golf, the Second World War (in which forty Pyramid Lake Paiutes left the reservation to fight, and came back to find their case still a Bleak House), the death of Roosevelt, the Truman administrations, the rise and decline of Senator McCarthy, and bebop. Miss Bowler was therefore less impressed than I with McCarran's professed surrender, but, like the Paiutes, she said it was a good sign. She drove me to the airport at Burbank to get my Las Vegas plane, and on the way over she gave me a copy of a memorandum she had drawn up in 1939 on the Pyramid Lake Indian land controversy. I read it on the plane. It was comprehensive, succinct, conclusive, irrefutable, and highly interesting, but it couldn't grow alfalfa.

Last March, after I had been back in New York for several months, I thought I would go down to Washington to see how McCarran was getting along on his new lacustrine tack. Before my talk with the Senator in Reno, the situation had seemed relatively simple—the unretreating old man pushing his ninth bill in sixteen years; the Indians resisting him, as always. The new administration, I had heard, was taking about the same line on Indian reservations as on oil reserves; it was out to liquidate them as rapidly as possible, and this, I had thought, might favor the old *caudillo's* ancient scheme. Now, after McCarran's professed abandonment of the cause, it seemed that the Indians were sure of a tie, at worst, but the settlers, with their water rights, had *them* blocked. It was up to McCarran to pick the lock of the United States Treasury for the benefit of both sides. He had long since forfeited the Indian vote in the Pyramid Lake region; if he failed in this, he would lose his state's Italian vote, too. To the Senator, remembering that he owed the last ten years of his glory to an almost imperceptible margin of votes in the 1944 Democratic primary, the outlook must have seemed grave. (He wouldn't be able to naturalize the most recent contingent of three hundred and eighty-five Basques in time to get any help from them.)

At the Bureau of Indian Affairs, on the fourth floor of a wing of the cavernous Department of the Interior Building, on C Street, a new Commissioner—Glenn Emmons, of Gallup, New Mexico—was in charge, and he had brought with him a new crew of assistants. An obliging, young public-relations man had told me over the telephone that he would scare up all the information he could on Pyramid Lake and have it ready when I arrived. Since Washington offers fewer inducements to walk slowly than Reno, I wasn't long in showing up, but even so, by the time I got there, the public-relations man had a pair of the Bureau's new young lawyers on hand, along with an old Indian Bureau irrigation man called Bill Miller. Miller had been over the ditches at the lake a dozen times; he knew all about the ditching and pumping side of the problem.

I didn't need them to tell me that the Indian Bureau was having a rough time. The 1953 session of Congress had passed an act enabling any state to assume civil and criminal jurisdiction over Indian reservations, formerly subject only to federal law, "at such time and in such manner as the people of the State shall, by affirmative legislative action, obligate and bind the State to assumption thereof." This put Indians pretty much at the mercy of the local authorities, from whom practically all previous federal Indian legislation had been designed to protect them. (The President, at the time he signed the bill, had called it "a most un-Christian approach to the problem" and expressed "grave doubts" about it. Nevertheless, he signed it, with a recommendation that Congress at its next session, in 1954, amend the act to require preliminary "consultation" with the tribes concerned and with the federal government. It has yet to be amended.) To make matters more difficult, the House had authorized the Committee on Interior and Insular Affairs to investigate the Indian Bureau with a view to drafting legislative proposals designed "to promote the earliest practicable termination of all Federal supervision and control over Indians," to transfer from the Bureau to the states as many functions as possible, to wind up the Bureau's activities in as many states as possible, and, in general, to absorb the Indians by abandonment, in the good old General Allotment Act fashion. As a reminder of the new policy, the Indian Bureau people had before them, on page 201 of the 1953–54 *United States Government Organization Manual,* this Congressional injunction: "The ultimate goal of the Bureau is to abolish the need for its own existence." This was generally being interpreted to mean, "The nearly immediate goal should be to fold before the cops arrive." An extreme example of the prevailing tendency was manifest in a bill introduced by Senator Malone, the junior Senator from Nevada, to "emancipate" the Indians by selling off all tribal assets within three years, which would constitute the greatest forced sale of lands and mineral rights in recorded history and would, of course, realize only an infinitesimal portion of the properties' true value. Malone wanted to whack up the proceeds among the tribe members, and then turn them loose. Concurrently, flocks of Western senators were offering bills to emancipate the Indians of various states and tribes from their holdings, and in most cases the Indians were resisting emancipation. A few tribes with high per-capita wealth were eager to be emancipated, but the solons who had these particular Indians as constituents seemed to feel that they should submit to further doses of administration, which included the leasing of their lumber and mineral rights, without their consent. To qualify for emancipation, an Indian, in the view of his Congressional friends, should be stripped as clean as a dressed turkey in a supermarket.

Such being the atmosphere of Washington, it did not seem likely to me that even old Pat could wangle money from Congress to buy *more* land for any Indians. "While we are spending billions of dollars fighting Communism and Marxist Socialism throughout the world, we are at the same time, through the Indian Bureau, perpetuating the systems of Indian reservations and tribal government, which are natural Socialist environments," the inimitable Malone had told the Senate. In view of Malone's position, how could the senior Senator from Nevada ask his colleague to add to the communal wealth?

The Indian Bureau fellows said that a Deputy Commissioner was out in Nevada right at that moment looking over the situation, and that they had requested the Army Engineers, as a third party, to make a new appraisal of the settlers' patent lands, ditches, and improvements; the trouble was, as we all knew, that the Engineers couldn't be expected to appraise nuisance value. At this stage of our talk, I delicately adumbrated a hypothetical question: If the Engineers' appraisal proved unacceptable to the settlers, and if the settlers' demands proved more than the new Commissioner, trying to make a reputation as a good administrator, felt he could endorse, or if they remained beyond what even McCarran thought he could manage, would the government, on behalf of the Indians, take legal action to secure to them the right to use the ditches on their own lands? On that, the Bureau people thought, I had better see the Bureau's new chief counsel, Harry A. Sellery, Jr., who was even then reading up on the Pyramid Lake case. "He sent for a summary this morning, and they brought him up half a ton of books," one of the young lawyers said.

A couple of days later, when I saw Mr. Sellery, he appeared mildly depressed, as if suffering from a headache caused by eyestrain. He said it appeared that his predecessors in the legal department of the Department of the Interior had requested that the Department of Justice take some suitable action, but that after a correspondence that must have been quite leisurely (each exchange of letters consumed the time it would take to raise four crops of alfalfa), Justice had expressed grave doubts about the outcome of such litigation. Mr. Sellery could not reveal to me the basis of these doubts, because to make them public might alert Sidney Robinson, the attorney for the squatters, to the flaws in the suit Justice wasn't bringing. I asked Mr. Sellery how much the Pyramid Lake case had cost the government already, and he replied, "About a million dollars."

I then got in touch with Mr. Miller, a friendly soul, and asked him if the irrigation engineers had ever calculated the cost of building a parallel system, by which the Indians could introduce *their* water from the river. (They have a right to more water than they use on their lands in the Truckee delta.) He said they had, they had. The cost had been estimated at a hundred and ninety thousand dollars. That gave me a clue to what the settlers' price would be.

At about this point in my investigations, a note from Harry Drackert was forwarded to me in Washington, enclosing good news in the form of a clipping from the *Nevada State Journal*, which started off with the four-column headline: FISHING IS BACK AT PYRAMID LAKE; GIANT-SIZED RAINBOW TROUT CAUGHT

The story was attributed to Ty Cobb, the *Journal's* sports editor, and it began:

> In Pyramid Lake—that vast body of water in the desert an hour's drive from Reno, supposedly "dead" for fishing this past quarter-century—they're catching trout! . . . In brief, here's the story: Giant-sized rainbow, apparently originally from the upper Truckee River, are being caught from the shore on the highway side of Pyramid Lake. The season is now on, as the state commission recently voted a year-round opening. If you're ready to make a dash for Pyramid Lake today, don't forget to get your state fishing license and also the special Indian permit which is absolutely required for this body of water. And the limit is five fish, in possession.

The state fish-and-game-commission men, Mr. Cobb wrote, had been trying for years to revive the fishing in the lake, working closely with the resources committee of the Pyramid Lake Indians, of which three Paiutes—Warren Tobey, Albert Aleck, and Ted James—were members. This hardly squared with the stories I had heard in Nevada in 1949—that the "shiftless" Indians had refused to *let* the game commission restock their lake. The commission had planted fry of the Kokanee salmon in 1951, but it was too early for results, since the Kokanee is a fish with a four-year cycle. It had also planted fry of the cutthroat trout in 1953, but this didn't account for the present catches of "huge rainbow trout—some as long as twenty-six inches and weighing close to ten pounds." The female fish were loaded with spawn, Mr. Cobb continued, and with this supply the commission men expected to raise thousands of fry of a strain that had obviously thrived for several years in the lake in order to attain that size. Mr. Cobb again:

> Where did the rainbows come from? Both Trelease [a commission fisheries man] and Warren Tobey think the big flood of 1950 and the high waters of the following winter must have washed the trout down from the upper Truckee River into the lake. The feed in the lake must be ideal for the rainbows,

because of about 25 taken by net or by hook, the majority were above five pounds in weight. . . . The Pyramid Lake Indians have given excellent coöperation all the way through on the programs now under way. They have aided in the planting activities, seining operations, and in drawing up the present agreement.

In deep summer, as the end of the Congressional session was approaching, I received a telephone call from the public-relations man of the Bureau of Indian Affairs. He said the Interior Department had struck a bargain with Mrs. De Paoli. She would accept thirty-one thousand dollars for her hundred and sixty acres of patent land, along with the buildings on it and the two ditches that brought water to it from the Truckee and then went north—dry—through four hundred acres or so of repossessed land. Now all McCarran had to do was get the money. Ceresola, on the other hand, was holding out. He wouldn't come down on his price.

A week or so later, a telegram arrived from the Indian Bureau informing me that Pat had introduced a bill for a supplemental appropriation for the Department of the Interior, including the thirty-one thousand dollars for Mrs. De Paoli, and that it had passed both houses. On August 27th, there was another telegram:

PRESIDENT YESTERDAY SIGNED SUPPLEMENTAL
APPROPRIATION INCLUDING 31,000 DOLLARS FOR
PURCHASE DE PAOLI INTERESTS PYRAMID LAKE
M M TOZIER INFORMATION OFFICER

The bill must have been one of the last the Senator introduced. Things had been going badly for him out in Nevada. The Democratic nomination for Governor had just been won by an old political enemy—Vail Pittman, younger brother of the Key Pittman who had overshadowed McCarran's first years in the Senate. When Key Pittman, who was chairman of the Senate Foreign Relations Committee, died of a heart attack in 1940, shortly after his sixth election to the Senate, Vail had taken his place as leader of an anti-McCarran faction. Eight years younger than McCarran, he had opposed him in the Senatorial primary of 1944. That was the one in which McCarran squeaked through by an almost imperceptible margin. After that, Pittman got himself elected Governor for a four-year term in 1946. When he ran for reëlection in 1950, McCarran worked against him, and Pittman was beaten. The Senator's beneficiary, a young Republican named Charlie Russell, had proved ungratefully hard to handle, though. Now, in 1954, Pittman seemed likely to beat Russell in the coming election. Either result would leave McCarran in a difficult position. At home, his hereditary rival, if elected Governor, would control the state machine and minimize McCarran's chances for renomination to the Senate in 1956. Furthermore, in Washington, McCarran could not look forward to having any federal patronage to hand out during the rest of the Eisenhower administration, for his support of McCarthy had isolated him from both the Democrats and the administration. The old man's only remaining Senatorial allies were the Jenners and Welkers—a splinter faction. He also had the reverential support of the Hearst press, whose nearest paper to Nevada is published in San Francisco, and of the Chicago *Tribune* and the New York *Daily News.* Hurrying home to make his peace with the Nevada Democrats, he had had to go out and beg for votes for Pittman—a humiliating test of his new amiability. (The eventual result of the election, a numbing surprise, was that Pittman got beaten, but hardly anybody would have predicted this in August.)

When I saw the *Times* headline:

SENATOR MCCARRAN IS DEAD IN NEVADA

under the usual libellous photograph, I noted that the dateline on the story was Hawthorne, which is a dismal town under a bleak mountain a hundred miles or so southeast of Reno. Hawthorne is the site of an enormous naval ammunition depot, which was put there because an explosion would cause less damage in that region than anywhere else in the United States. The population of the town is eighteen hundred. You can see Hawthorne from the plane that carries you between Las Vegas and Reno; the plane is a DC-3, and if there is a passenger for Hawthorne it puts down there. I knew that McCarran, because of his heart condition, never flew. To make a speech at Hawthorne, he must have had to travel two or three hours by automobile over a baking desert road. The dispatch read, in part: "The white-haired veteran collapsed as he was walking down a side aisle after addressing some 125 persons at the Civic Centre in this Western Nevada town."

A typical Nevada rhubarb followed, even before they got McCarran to the cathedral at Reno, where the Roman Catholic Bishop of Reno pronounced the eulogy. The Republican Governor Russell claimed the right to name a senator to fill out the old man's term, which had until December, 1956, to run. The State Attorney General, a Democrat, said that Nevada law required both parties to nominate Senatorial candidates, who would be voted on at the forthcoming election. Such nominations would have to be filed a month before Election Day, which meant almost instantly. The Republicans protested that they would appeal to the State Supreme Court, but they went ahead and picked a candidate anyway, because they couldn't afford to be without one if the court turned them down. There were hurried, violent intra-party squabbles. The mood was wrong for a really good funeral. As I read of these ructions, I recalled the fierce old man saying, "You can't win 'em all." I think that that admission was the beginning of the end.

Appendix

The maps in this appendix will enlarge readers' understanding of the information presented in this book.

Both the Pyramid Lake and Walker River Indian Reservations were created by the federal government in 1859, when the lands surrounding both lakes were withdrawn from the public domain and designated as Indian reservations. The initial map in this appendix is the first map of the Pyramid Lake Indian Reservation. In 1864 a surveyor named Eugene Monroe surveyed the Walker River Reservation and drew a map of it; in 1865 he did the same thing for the reservation at Pyramid Lake. The so-called Monroe map played a role in establishing the right of the Pyramid Lake Paiutes to ownership of the disputed lands discussed in this book, because it established that the reservation was clearly described years before issuance of an 1874 executive order ratifying the earlier action. This map was copied from the Records of the Nevada District Court at the Federal Records Center–San Francisco.

The next two maps were drawn by Karen Laramore and are based on maps in the Robert Leland Collection in the Special Collections Department, University of Nevada, Reno Library. They are used here by permission of the Special Collections Department, University of Nevada, Reno Library.

The map of the reservation as it was in 1934 indicates that the overall size and shape of the reservation had not changed since the 1860s, even though valuable land within these boundaries had been lost to non-Indians.

The third map shows the lands recovered by the Pyramid Lake Paiute Tribe through the litigation described in this book. This controversy involved most of the lands occupied by non-Indians within this portion of the reservation.

The final map shows the lands actually used for agricultural purposes within the lower part of the reservation, as of early 1999. The lands labeled "Garaventa/DePaoli" in the lower left-hand corner of the map comprise the last portions of the disputed lands recovered by the Tribe. This ranch was purchased as a result of provisions of the Negotiated Settlement discussed in the introduction. Although not precisely comparable with the preceding map because it shows lands actually farmed rather than ownership patterns, the map shows that the lands occupied by the squatters were among the most valuable agricultural lands in this portion of the reservation. This map was also adapted by Karen Laramore from a map supplied by John Jackson, Director of Water Resources of the Pyramid Lake Paiute Tribe.

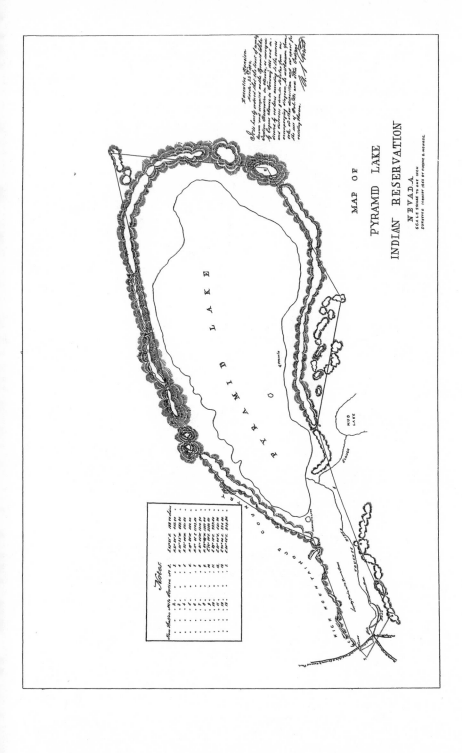

MAP OF
PYRAMID LAKE
INDIAN RESERVATION
NEVADA.

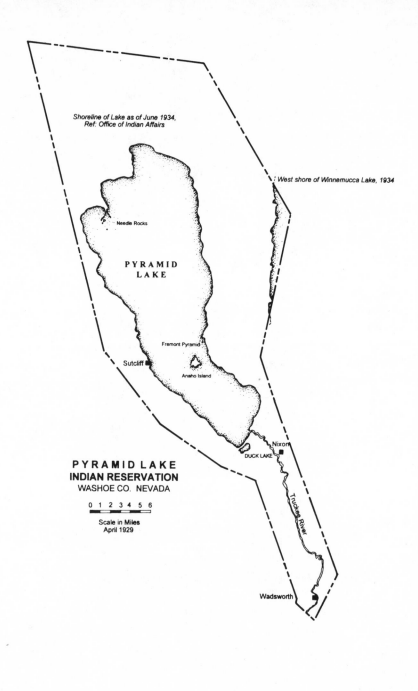

Shoreline of Lake as of June 1934,
Ref: Office of Indian Affairs

West shore of Winnemucca Lake, 1934

Needle Rocks

PYRAMID
LAKE

Fremont Pyramid

Sutcliff

Anaho Island

Nixon

DUCK LAKE

Truckee River

PYRAMID LAKE
INDIAN RESERVATION
WASHOE CO. NEVADA

0 1 2 3 4 5 6

Scale in Miles
April 1929

Wadsworth

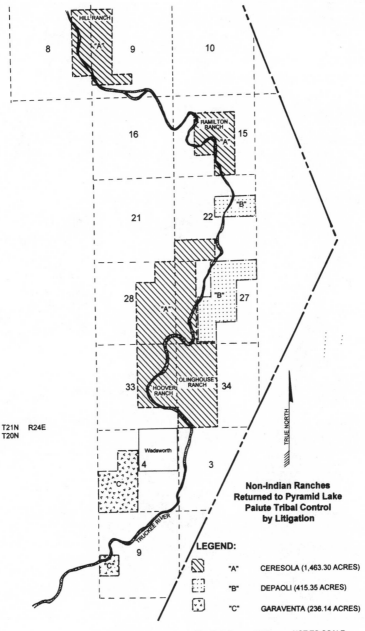

T21N R24E
T20N

**Non-Indian Ranches
Returned to Pyramid Lake
Paiute Tribal Control
by Litigation**

LEGEND:

"A"   CERESOLA (1,463.30 ACRES)

"B"   DEPAOLI (415.35 ACRES)

"C"   GARAVENTA (236.14 ACRES)

After C. J. Freece, 1945.   NOT TO SCALE

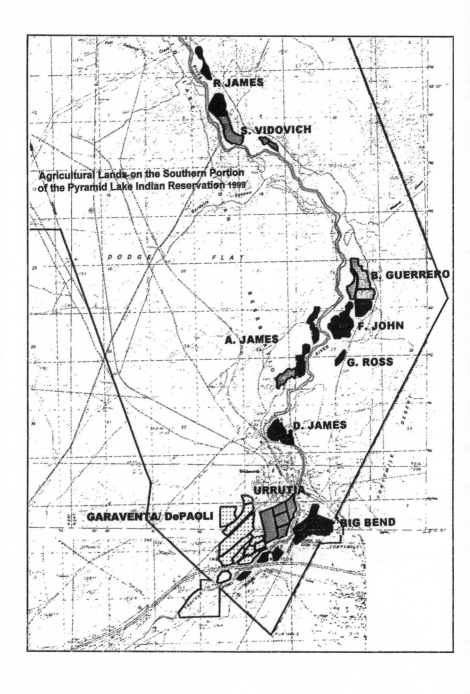

Agricultural Lands on the Southern Portion
of the Pyramid Lake Indian Reservation 1999

R. JAMES

S. VIDOVICH

B. GUERRERO

F. JOHN

A. JAMES

G. ROSS

D. JAMES

URRUTIA

GARAVENTA DePAOLI

BIG BEND

A Note on Sources About Pyramid Lake

There is a substantial literature about Pyramid Lake and related topics. The starting point for further reading in this area must be Alvin R. McLane, *Pyramid Lake: A Bibliography* (Reno: Camp Nevada, 1975). Although now outdated, McLane's bibliography is annotated and thorough. For example, it includes some hard-to-find newspaper articles.

Another general source is an issue of the *Nevada Public Affairs Review* published in 1992 by the Alan Bible Center for Applied Research at the University of Nevada, Reno. *Dividing Desert Waters*, edited by Peter Goin, Robert Dawson, and Jill M. Winter, contains articles and illustrations on a wide range of topics (the most important of which are listed separately below). This publication contains some of the best recent information about the lake.

Anthropologists have produced a great deal of scholarly literature about Great Basin Indians, including the Pyramid Lake Paiutes, although typically the literature is focused on the period before Euro-American intrusion. Literature on Native Americans of the Great Basin is summarized and analyzed in the *Great Basin* volume of the Smithsonian Institution's *Handbook of North American Indians,* published in 1986. This volume is the basic one for anyone seeking information about Great Basin Indians. Pyramid Lake Paiutes are dealt with in the *Handbook* chapter on Northern Paiutes by Sven Liljeblad and Catherine S. Fowler (pp. 412–34), but there are also several specific references to Pyramid Lake Paiutes at other places in this basic reference work.

Since the *Great Basin Handbook,* there have been several works on the Pyramid Lake Paiutes. One of the most important is the publication by Catherine Fowler listed below, the first of two volumes that will make accessible the field notes of anthropologist Willard Z. Park, who did extensive work at Pyramid Lake in the 1930s. *As Long as the River Shall Run,* by Martha C. Knack and Omer C. Stewart, summarizes (mainly from U.S. government documents) the history of interactions between the Pyramid Lake

Paiutes and Euro-Americans since the middle of the nineteenth century. The book by Nellie Harnar gives a brief history of the Tribe from the standpoint of one of its members.

That Was Happy Life is an award-winning video tribute to the life of Katie Frazier, a member of the Pyramid Lake Paiute Tribe who died in 1991 at the age of one hundred. Produced by Jo Anne Peden, it is available from the Teaching and Learning Technologies Office of the University of Nevada, Reno; proceeds from its sale go to the Katie Frazier Native American Scholarship at UNR. *Healing the Water* is an excellent video produced in 1997 by the Water Education Foundation, Box 50, Sacramento, California 95812.

Dividing Desert Waters provides much information about recent legal/governmental efforts to save Pyramid Lake, although a full account of these efforts has yet to be written. Parts of this legal history are still in court records and the files and memories of the major participants. The Special Collections Department of the Getchell Library, University of Nevada, Reno, has many legal and other materials about the lake's recent history. Several items listed below give information on various aspects of the legal conflicts, particularly the dispute between California and Nevada, which is given little attention here. An excellent series on the activities leading to the Negotiated Settlement, written by Doug McMillan and Don Vetter, appeared in the *Reno Gazette-Journal* from August 21 to August 26, 1988. Faith Bremner of this newspaper has covered water issues in northwestern Nevada with great skill for several years.

There is also a substantial technical literature on topics ranging from hydrological studies to detailed biological reports. A few of the items listed below deal in nontechnical fashion with some of these questions.

Books

California Department of Water Resources. *Truckee River Atlas.* Sacramento: California Department of Water Resources, 1991.

Fowler, Catherine S. *Willard Z. Park's Ethnographic Notes on the Northern Paiute of Western Nevada, 1933–1934.* Vol. 1. Salt Lake City: University of Utah Anthropological Papers, No. 114, 1989.

Harnar, Nellie Shaw. *Indians of Coo-yu-ee Pah (Pyramid Lake): The History of the Pyramid Lake Indians.* Sparks, Nev.: Western Printing and Publishing Co., 1978.

Horton, Gary A. *Truckee River Chronology: A Chronological History of the Truckee River and Related Water Issues.* Seventh Update. Carson City: Division of Water Planning, Department of Conservation and Natural Resources, 1997.

Jackson, W. Turrentine, and Donald J. Pisani. *A Case Study in Interstate Resource Management: The California-Nevada Water Controversy, 1865–1955.* Davis, Calif.: California Water Resources Center, Publication No. 142, 1973.

———. *A Case Study in Interstate Resource Management: The California-Nevada Water Controversy, 1955–1968.* Davis, Calif.: California Water Resources Center, Publication No. 147, 1979.

Knack, Martha C., and Omer C. Stewart. *As Long as the River Shall Run: An Ethnohistory of the Pyramid Lake Indian Reservation.* Berkeley: University of California Press, 1984; Reno: University of Nevada Press, 1999.

Minckley, W. L., and James E. Deacon, eds. *Battle Against Extinction: Native Fish Management in the American West.* Tucson: University of Arizona Press, 1991.

Pisani, Donald J. *To Reclaim a Divided West: Water, Law, and Public Policy, 1848–1902.* Albuquerque: University of New Mexico Press, 1992.

Sierra Pacific Power Company. *1985–2005 Water Resources Plan.* 6 vols. Reno: Sierra Pacific Power Company, 1985.

Townley, John M. *The Orr Ditch Case, 1913–1944.* Publication No. 43007. Reno: University of Nevada, Reno, Desert Research Institute, Water Resources Center, 1980.

Westpac Utilities. *Water Resource Plan, 1988–2008.* Reno: Sierra Pacific Power Company, 1989.

Articles

D'Agostini, Daniel. "At the End of a River." *Pacific Discovery* (Jan.–Mar. 1987): 6–19.

Ely, Joe. "More Than Romance." In Peter Goin, Robert Dawson, and Jill M. Winter (eds.), *Dividing Desert Waters, Nevada Public Affairs Review* 1 (Reno: University of Nevada, Reno, Senator Alan Bible Center for Applied Research, 1992): 60–63.

Gammon, Clive. "Lost and Found: A Fish Story." *Sports Illustrated,* 6 November 1989.

Janik, C. Anne, and Ronald M. Anglin. "Nevada's Unique Wildlife Oasis." In Peter Goin, Robert Dawson, and Jill M. Winter (eds.), *Dividing Desert Waters, Nevada Public Affairs Review* 1 (Reno: University of Nevada, Reno, Senator Alan Bible Center for Applied Research, 1992): 54–59.

Nappe, Tina. "Negotiating the Future of Wildlife: Saving Wetlands and Fish Along the Truckee River." Bend, Ore.: High Desert Museum, 1991.

Rowley, William G. "The Newlands Project: Crime or National Commitment." In Peter Goin, Robert Dawson, and Jill M. Winter (eds.), *Dividing Desert Waters, Nevada Public Affairs Review* 1 (Reno: University of Nevada, Reno, Senator Alan Bible Center for Applied Research, 1992): 39–49.

Rusco, Elmer R. "Formation of the Pyramid Lake Paiute Tribal Council, 1934–1936." *Journal of California and Great Basin Anthropology* 10, no. 22 (1988): 187–208.

———. "The Truckee–Carson–Pyramid Lake Water Rights Settlement Act and Pyramid Lake." In Peter Goin, Robert Dawson, and Jill M. Winter (eds.), *Dividing Desert Waters, Nevada Public Affairs Review* 1 (Reno: University of Nevada, Reno, Senator Alan Bible Center for Applied Research, 1992): 9–15.

Scoppettone, G. Gary, Mark Coleman, and Gary A. Wedemeyer. "Life History and Status of the Endangered Cui-ui of Pyramid Lake, Nevada." *Fish and Wildlife Research* 1 (1986).

Strickland, Rose. "Stillwater: Its Friends and Neighbors." In Peter Goin, Robert Dawson, and Jill M. Winter (eds.), *Dividing*

Desert Waters, Nevada Public Affairs Review 1 (Reno: University of Nevada, Reno, Senator Alan Bible Center for Applied Research, 1992): 68–73.

Webb, Mary. "Pyramid Lake: The Tonic of Wilderness." In Peter Goin, Robert Dawson, and Jill M. Winter (eds.), *Dividing Desert Waters, Nevada Public Affairs Review* 1: 50–53.

Wilds, Leah J., Danny A. Gonzalez, and Glen S. Krutz. "Reclamation and the Politics of Change: The Truckee–Carson–Pyramid Lake Water Rights Settlement Act." *Nevada Historical Society Quarterly* 37, 3 (1994): 173–99.

Unpublished Sources

Dixon, Faun Mortara. "Native American Property Rights: The Pyramid Lake Reservation Land Controversy." Ph.D. diss., University of Nevada, Reno, 1981.

Haller, Timothy G. "California-Nevada Interstate Water Compact: A Study in Controversy." Ph.D. diss., University of Nevada, Reno, 1981.

Underdal, Stanley J. "On the Road Toward Termination: The Pyramid Lake Paiutes and the Indian Attorney Controversy of the 1950s." Ph.D. diss., Columbia University, 1977.